"There are a lot of books about what preaching is and how to preach, but there are fewer books that practically walk the preacher through how to prepare that sermon to preach. This is why I am grateful for this small, concise, and accessible book appropriately titled, *Simple Sermon*. Valenti walks you through his own approach to prepare a sermon that is clear, precise, and in a good and helpful way…simple. He has used this method to train men in his own ministry for many years. I believe this little book could help you in a similar way."

—**Brian Croft**
Executive Director
Practical Shepherding

"This is an excellent, simple and very practical book on preaching. There are multiple books out in the Church right now on this topic, but this one stands out as it walks us through text from sermon prep to finish. This cheeky little number is worth buying for yourself and for those hoping to be preachers, or improve their sermons.

It's not hard to see that I am the author's exegetical inspiration!"

—**Mez McConnell**
Executive Director 20schemes
Author, *Church in Hard Places* (and a ton of other books)

"Not only is Dr. Tony Valenti a dear friend and gift in my life, he is a faithful preacher of God's Word. Often times when you get to know someone you discern that there's some dissonance between what they espouse and what they live — not the case with Tony. What sets this book on preaching apart is that it's not just theory but I've seen his wisdom and approach to preaching week in and week out and have personally benefitted from it. I'm a more faithful preacher because of the words you'll read in this book. Whether you're a seasoned preacher or just starting out this simple, wise, and practical book on preaching will serve you well."

—**Dr. Nathan Millican**
Pastor Graceland Church
Author, *Before We Forget*

DR. TONY VALENTI

SIMPLE

SERMONS

How to Write Faster, Stress Less, and
Preach Better Sermons **in Three Days**

Simple Sermons
How to Write Faster, Stress Less, and Preach Better Sermons in Three Days
Copyright © 2025 by Dr. Tony Valenti

Published by Lucid Books in Houston, TX
www.LucidBooks.com

All rights reserved. No part of this publication may be reproduced, stored in a retrieval system, or transmitted in any form by any means, electronic, mechanical, photocopy, recording, or otherwise, without the prior permission of the publisher, except as provided for by USA copyright law.

Unless otherwise indicated, scripture quotations are taken from the ESV® Bible (The Holy Bible, English Standard Version®), copyright © 2001 by Crossway, a publishing ministry of Good News Publishers. Used by permission. All rights reserved.

Scripture quotations marked (CSB) are from the Holman Christian Standard Bible®, Copyright © 2017 by Holman Bible Publishers. Used by permission.

ISBN: 978-1-63296-832-6 (paperback)
ISBN: 978-1-63296-833-3 (hardback)
eISBN: 978-1-63296-834-0

Special Sales: Most Lucid Books titles are available in special quantity discounts. Custom imprinting or excerpting can also be done to fit special needs. Contact Lucid Books at Info@LucidBooks.com

This book is dedicated to my wonderful Godly wife, Andrea, and two fantastic kids, Tony and Gracie.

Thank you for encouraging me and giving me the time to write this book. I could not have asked for a better family.

Table of Contents

Foreword		1
Introduction		13
Chapter 1	The Toyota Corolla of Sermon Books	17
Chapter 2	What is a Sermon?	21
Chapter 3	A Three-Day Plan	29
	Day One Monday	
Chapter 4	Starting Your Day	37
Chapter 5	Pray and Meditate on the Word	41
Chapter 6	Verse Diagram	43
Chapter 7	Exegetical Outline	49
Chapter 8	Applicational Outline	53
Chapter 9	Resources	59
Chapter 10	Answer the Questions	63
	Day Two Tuesday	
Chapter 11	The Holy Spirit and the Sermon Writer	69
Chapter 12	Sermon Outline	71
Chapter 13	Organize	75
Chapter 14	The Case for the Big Idea	79
Chapter 15	Subpoints Explanation	89
Chapter 16	Subpoints Application	101
Chapter 17	Next Steps	109
	Day Three Wednesday	
Chapter 18	Why Spend a Day on Coloring?	121
Chapter 19	Intro and Outro	133
Chapter 20	Rest and Preach!	139
Chapter 21	What Do I Do on Sunday?	141
Chapter 22	You Did It!	145
Chapter 23	The Stuff at the End	149
Appendix I	Standing on the Shoulders of Giants	167
Appendix II	Pray Psalm 119	169

Foreword

A few words from people who use this process

> Every pastor wants to communicate well. Every pastor wants to preach well. Every pastor wants to make most of the time that he has. It is because of this that many men enter seminary each year. But seminary only taught me so much. I needed the practical week in and week out of sermon preparation. As I left the halls of academia and began weekly preaching and teaching God's word, I realized the gaps I had in knowledge and practice. After studying at a Bible college and seminary, I had gathered many tools to preach God's word. Through taking classes in hermeneutics, exegesis, and homiletics, I had learned the foundational principles of studying God's Word and communicating it to others. But one of the most important aspects of preaching is the ability to take God's Word and craft a sermon.

Simple Sermons

Since we want to communicate well, pastors like me spend hours on end preparing and crafting our sermons. But because preaching is only one aspect in the role of the pastor, we must learn how to make the most use of our time. By using the tools in this book, I was able to cut my sermon prep time in half. That does not mean that I needed to cut corners, instead, I learned how to use the same pattern and form every week to prepare the sermon. By integrating a preaching preparation document in which I diagram the passage, utilize an exegetical outline, and then an application outline, I can clearly, concisely, and cogently analyze the scripture text before sitting down and writing the sermon. Tony Valenti has helped me to execute this task much quicker. This has helped me gain more time to pastor the congregants in my local church, while at the same time respectfully handling God's Word and delivering messages that apply God's Word to our daily lives.

I can fully endorse this book, and I recommend it to all pastors that desire to preach God's word faithfully while at the same time use their time as wisely as possible for the Kingdom of God. This is especially important to those that are bi-vocational or co-vocational. I am thankful to have spent time learning the skills in this book, and I am encouraged that it will pay dividends for decades to come.

Erick Sessions
Campus Pastor • Graceland
Salem, Indiana

Foreword

When I started in ministry 14 years ago, I had taken a preaching class in school, but I didn't have a consistent method for preparing sermons, which is probably why I only preached six times in my first 12 years of ministry. Without reps and a strategy, it felt like every time I was asked to preach, I had to relearn how to write a sermon.

I started a residency two years ago under the guidance of Tony Valenti. I became a campus pastor but had minimal preaching experience. The first thing Tony showed me was how to think like a preacher, using this process.

My sermons turned from mere academic exercises of exegeting a text to having God's Word wash over and minister to me. Ministry is busy, and when you believe you have mastered a sermon-building process, it can be easy to shorten the heart preparation steps because you wrongly believe that no one sees that. God sees it, and it shows up in your delivery. While serving as a campus pastor, I am also completing my seminary studies. There have been weeks, especially with papers due, books to read, and finals to study for, that I have skimped on the heart preparation. I feel it on a Sunday after I step down from the pulpit, but in the weeks when I don't skip the heart preparation process, God always uses what I have prepared to minister to myself and His people.

Faithfully following these steps ensures that God's Word is correctly understood and reliable applications are made. The method has been a game changer for me as I prepare sermons. There are numerous excellent resources available to assist in the sermon preparation process, including commentaries, dictionaries, and word studies. However, you cannot start there. This process involves you personally interacting with the text, allowing you to share your unbiased thoughts. This is part of the process where I used to get overwhelmed because I didn't know where to start, but by simply reading the text and diagramming it, I now begin with a basic understanding of what the text says.

Tony's sermon preparation process includes two additional tools that have significantly shaped my preparation and execution. The second tool is his prep notes document. The following are questions or statements that shape the content of the message; the first is a big idea. At Graceland, the preaching pastors develop these together at a sermon prep retreat, and each campus works off of the same big idea each week. The next component I didn't initially understand is called "tweet the point." The purpose is to be able to capture the essence of the message in 280 characters or less.

The next point is what command is God calling us to. After that came context. This section is so helpful because it is where you can explain any unique elements of a text without disrupting the flow of the message. The following four parts force me to know what I want to say as I preach. The first question is, "What would people lose if this text wasn't there." Essentially, this question helps me understand why God would take the time to have an author convey this information. At Graceland we preach Christocentric messages, and because of this, every message I preach needs to have a tie to and proclamation of the gospel.

Foreword

This next question practically helps me navigate the length of the message and the position of certain elements it is "What are the additional service components?" Considering service elements allows me to shape my message to fit the audience. I make my illustrations family friendly on family Sundays. I also adjust the length of my message for the sake of children and their parents. The next element is which of our church's core values I will incorporate into the sermon. The final component is what are my application points. Weekly creating this prep document enables me to share and receive feedback during our sermon preparation meetings.

The last document Tony has is a breakdown of how long it should take to prepare a message. By far, this has been my greatest struggle, especially being in seminary, maintaining a healthy marriage, having a great relationship with my four kids, and shepherding a flock. Initially, I would spend over 20 hours preparing a sermon. I felt like I was drowning and accomplishing nothing. Since I was spending so much time on my message, there were weeks when I wouldn't finish until Saturday evening, having spent the entire week working on it. Tony's sermon prep breakdown is not rocket science. It takes diligence, patience, and a good kick in the pants by a boss who cares about you and your family to get your sermon prep time to an appropriate length. The following is the general breakdown I use each time I prepare a sermon. Day 1 – Verse diagram, exegetical outline, applicational outline, and research, which takes approximately three hours. Day 2 – I write the outline of my sermon, which takes about four hours. Day 3 –

Simple Sermons

I color my sermon with illustrations, which takes about 2 hours. Having this breakdown and forcing myself to be accountable for it has helped me love my family and flock

Jake Shipe
Campus Pastor • Graceland
Salem, Indiana

> I have ministered in both small and medium churches over the last two and half decades, occupying a variety of roles from youth pastor to lead pastor to church planter; and I've collected my fair share of resources on how to become more effective in sermon writing. However, few of those resources served to move the needle of my writing effectiveness, which is why Dr. Tony Valenti's book Simple Sermons is refreshing, as well as a must-own resource for any pastor.

Early in my ministry, sermon writing brought great excitement but had little direction. After days and days of reading, writing, re-reading, and re-writing – all my sermon preparations felt like a pile of gunpowder; there was powerful potential but no way to narrow the focus and impact. Ultimately, my sermons ended up all over the place with no clear application, resulting in a common refrain from the church asking, "So what?" or "What's next?"

The applicational heart of the text was often overshadowed by the exegetical head. But it also worked the other way around, as I could easily focus solely on the application at the sake of solid,

Foreword

biblical exegesis. Working with Dr. Valenti and the process he lays out for joining together the exegetical and applicational has transformed my preaching. Starting with an exegetical outline and then building an applicational outline has taken the loose pile of gunpowder and packed it into a delivery mechanism that is on target and reaches the heart of the congregation with both focus and impact!

Across decades of ministry, I have also learned first-hand that people (including myself) can only ingest and digest so much information at one time. With Dr. Valenti's guidance, my ability to simplify the biblical text down to a big idea has been perhaps the single greatest way I've been able to serve my church well. I have realized that the people who hear my sermons don't remember my "finely-crafted" and "well-alliterated" points by the time they reach the parking lot; but if I can give them a single and clear call from the text (i.e., the big idea), that is something they can take with them and act upon. The ability to distill the text into its main thrust, as it relates to the overarching story of God's redemptive plan for mankind, has been my key to unlocking the remainder of my study and preparation.

Using Dr. Valenti's process to identify the big idea also forces me to simplify the text so that I can explain it to an 8-year-old who wants to come to Christ, or to an 88-year-old who has only recently come to faith in Christ. Identifying the big idea of the text is like locating the North Star; once you know where it is, it is easy to follow, and it keeps you on track. The big idea always comes from the biblical text, never the daily headlines; however,

Simple Sermons

I can make relevant applicational points because they spring from the big idea through careful exegesis.

Dr. Valenti's book also addresses one of the biggest challenges for any pastor and that is time. Afterall, there are only 24 hours in a day, and ministry often requires the use of all of those hours – plus some. As a pastor of a medium-sized church in the Southern Baptist Convention, my time is regularly split into more slices than a pecan pie at a church potluck. Yet, preaching is my main calling and responsibility, which not only requires time – but focused and intentional time. The better I become at drawing out the main idea and its supporting structure, the quicker I can build a message that captures the heart of the text and that resonates with my people. This in turn frees me up to minister to the congregation beyond the pews on Sunday morning. I've been blessed by Dr. Valenti's processes which have helped me to spend the appropriate time in the text before I spend the time writing, editing, and revising.

Dr. Valenti's book also provides helpful guidance when it comes to the actual "pen-to-paper" writing of sermons as he provides practical information on topics such as the development and use of illustrations in a sermon. I always felt my illustrations were serviceable, but after working with Dr. Valenti, my illustrations have been pushed farther and deeper in order to better connect with my audience. Instead of stopping short in my development, I'm encouraged to go "one level deeper" and to make sure my illustrations are personal, relatable, and powerful.

Foreword

I have been both challenged and encouraged in serving alongside and learning from Tony. His genuine love for faithful and powerful preaching is always on display, and his grasp of tools and techniques to elevate sermons to new heights is more than admirable. I can honestly say I am a better preacher thanks to his guidance, and I employ his processes each week as I seek to honor God with my sermons.

Ben McClain
Campus Pastor • Graceland
Memphis, Indiana

> One of the great joys in my life is preaching and studying preachers. The first time I listened to John Piper preach, I knew that's what I was called to do with my life. The problem was that I never had someone to teach me how to preach. Plenty of churches were kind enough to give me the opportunity, but no one explicitly taught me how to expound the Scripture in an edifying, productive, and clear way that builds up the Church.

My sermon prep process used to consist of reading the text, sifting through the theological implications of the text, and then finding the moral applications to fit at the end. To check myself, I listened to my favorite preachers and tried to emulate what the way they preached and how they formed their sermons. I always made sure I had three points that rhymed or had some

Simple Sermons

catchy alliteration, along with two moral applications at the end. Every preacher has their own system to prepare for and develop sermons, but when I listen to some of those sermons today, I'm amazed the Lord used any of it. When I look back at my notes of old sermons, I have so many more questions than what I'm sure I answered in the sermon itself. My sermons were overcomplicated and unclear.

I met Tony Valenti when he joined our pastoral team at Graceland Church. Armed with his extensive knowledge in training pastors, Tony and I met regularly to examine my sermons. He was supportively candid and analytical in his approach to carefully shape my ability to preach. This type of training was similar to Master Yoda training Luke Skywalker in The Empire Strikes back – there were a lot more things to fix than were going well – all because I was overcomplicating the process.

Tony explained how to preach Simple Sermons, sermons anyone could listen to, understand, and grow in some way. The goal was not to show people how amazing of a preacher I am, but to give them an amazing view of God in the clearest way possible. Complex sermon preparation leads to complex sermons that are hard to listen or learn from. Tony taught me a simpler way of preparing a sermon so that I am able to help listeners understand the Bible in a way that glorifies God and is faithful to the Bible. The goal of preaching is not to fill heads, but to change hearts and move people to follow Jesus.

An important lesson for me to learn was that complexity in preaching does not mean depth. Tony once told me, "You don't

Foreword

want your listeners going to lunch after church and saying, 'Pastor Bo is such a gifted preacher.' If that's the only part of your sermon their talking about, then we've missed. You want your people saying, 'Because Bo preached this passage, I understand the Bible a little bit better.'" The sermons are to edify the Church and make disciples who can go and share the gospel with the world. If I overcomplicate my sermons, I'm making disciples who can tell other people how awesome I am. That would be an epic failure. I want people sitting around their lunch tables talking about how amazing God is for what He has revealed about Himself in Scripture and how much it has changed their lives.

Today, I can go back and see my growth from my old system of preparation to the tactics that Tony taught. It has served my church in unspeakable ways as people are going from a common attender to an active member who is growing in their faith and knowledge of the Bible, all because the sermons are simple and clear. Paul wrote, "And I, when I came to you, brothers, did not come proclaiming to you the testimony of God with lofty speech or wisdom. For I decided to know nothing among you except Jesus Christ and Him crucified" (1 Corinthians 2:1-2). Paul's goal for preaching was for people to marvel at the beauty and power of God that has been revealed by Scripture. Let this be your goal as you seek to prepare to preach faithful sermons that change lives.

Tony's steps he proposes are not the magic, pragmatic secret to preaching but it has shaped and molded my preaching preparation in ways that have grown me as a preacher. My preparation starts with the initial reading and prayer over the text, then the sentence

Simple Sermons

diagram, which I will print and mark up a million times that will help me form exegetical and application outlines. This gives me a clear view of the big idea of the passage, and I begin write my exposition of the text and how it connects with my applicational points. The next step is to add the transitional phrases and illustrations. Finally, I write my introduction and conclusion. I trust this system to the point that by Saturday, I don't have to look over my sermon in fear of Sunday because the process has had the text of Scripture at the forefront of my mind leading up to the sermon.

When I first began using this process, I was skeptical that it was too simple and some of the elements were not necessary. I can truthfully say that the weeks I tried to cut corners are noticeable. When I follow the steps of the process faithfully, I feel free and confident because I know that I have done to work to preach the Bible directly to my listeners in a way that is clear, understandable, and applicable. The principles Pastor Tony has laid out in this book have changed my preaching ministry forever and my prayer is that they will do the same for you.

Bo Mangold
Campus Pastor • Graceland
Memphis, Indiana

Introduction

This book is for the preachers out there. The ones who are first starting and the ones toiling every week to get a sermon written in between hospital visits, Bible studies, business meetings, disgruntled people, and everything else that comes in the normal week of pastoring. Over the ten years I served as a lead pastor and every-week preacher, I found that my struggle was not with how to interpret and write the text, it was with the workflow of writing a sermon. This book shares how to write sermons while still pastoring your church effectively.

Most pastors I talk with or train have a similar problem. Their motivation is to write early, but the reality is that many resort to rushed research and writing at the end of the week. Many cannot get past rewording what other preachers and scholars have already written and preached. The "Saturday Night Special" becomes the norm. And because of this, their families and churches suffer. Many times, they lose a love for preaching and prepping. The joy

Pastoral Tip

Pastoring is more than preaching, but it is not less.

Introduction

of preaching is pulled from them and becomes another thing they must do. This does not just hurt them; it hurts their churches, too. In 2018, there was a popular meme of a horse going around. The front of the horse looked like it was drawn by a 5-year-old, and the back end of the horse looked like it was drawn by a professional artist.

The back end of the horse is a sermon started on Monday. It is researched, loved, and detailed. The picture is clear. But then church happens. Sally calls when her dad is in the hospital. Deacon Joe is unhappy that he got assigned to the wrong aisle on Sunday. Communion is coming, and you have no more juice cups. You have a Bible study you lead on Wednesdays that you need to prep for. And now it's Saturday. Part of the horse is clear, but you don't preach the back end of the horse. And so you rush, and the results are the front. The church does not see the back end of the horse. They only get the front end, and it's rough. But this does not have to be your process, pastor.

The goal of this book is to offer a simple system of sermon writing, a rhythm that is easily duplicated, so that you can enjoy the process and avoid the "Saturday Night Specials." The book is broken into three parts. Each part corresponds with a day of writing. At the end of this book, and with some practice, you should be able to write a clear Biblical sermon in three days. With this rhythm you won't present your churches with the front end of a half-drawn horse.

CHAPTER 1

The Toyota Corolla of Sermon Books

In 2009, I bought two Toyota Corollas. Why two? Because my wife and I both needed new cars. She was driving her car from high school, and I was driving an old beat-down truck. We were both working in the Phoenix metro and driving around forty miles a day each. I love the hunt for a car. This was when you would have to go to every dealer's website to find the right car. A friend of mine said we should check out a Lexus dealer because they sold newer Corollas from the service lot. I found a wealth of beautiful Corollas with less than 1,000 miles listed well under Blue Book value. So, I told my wife Andrea that I was going to pick one up. She, in her wisdom and grace, said, "why don't you just get two? We both need a car." And so I went to the dealership and said, "Give me two white Corollas." Done and done.

I know that you are *not* asking yourself, what was the top speed of those bad boys? Why do I know that? Because no one cares what the top speed of the Corolla is. The purpose of the

Tony's Life Tip
Look for the cheapest things at the most expensive places.

The Toyota Corolla of Sermon Books

Corolla is to get you somewhere as reliably as possible. Not to go fast. Not to look sexy. They exist to get you there. The sermon process in this book is the Toyota Corolla of sermon preparation. It is not sexy. It is consistent. It gets you from Point A to Point B. This process will provide you with a biblically sound, reliable, engaging, and faithful sermon every time. You can just call this book *Simple Sermon: the Toyota Corolla of Sermon Prep Books*.

Tony's Life Tip

If your wife gives you permission to buy something, do it right away. Don't miss the moment.

CHAPTER 2

What is a Sermon?

I f I went to my ninety-four-year-old grandpa and asked, "Did you watch that livestream last night?" He would be confused about the weird question, and his answer would probably include the words fish, water, lake, and forest. If I went to my thirty-year-old youth pastor and asked the same question, his answer would be focused on watching something on the internet. Why? Well, the word livestream has a different meaning for a ninety-four-year-old fisherman than they do for a slightly aging youth pastor. After watching hundreds of sermons and training many men on how to write sermons, I can say with confidence that we all do not share the same definition of the word sermon. So, before we get to the process, let's define sermon.

Pastoral Tip

The best way to ensure your church has a "high-view" of preaching is to preach well-prepared biblical sermons.

What is a Sermon?

As defined by me for this book, a sermon is a public address given to the church that adheres to the following rules:
- The Bible drives. In other words, it's expository.
- The speaker writes. We're going to do the work; we don't preach other people's words or ideas.
- It is applicational. Tell the people what they need to know and how to respond.
- It is empowered. Writing and preaching a sermon are acts empowered by the Holy Spirit.
- Jesus is center. The Bible points to Jesus. So should your sermon.

Many people will say many things on any given Sunday, but the sermon is special and set apart. We need to treat it that way.

This has not always been my approach. It's the end of my first year of ministry, and I finally get the ask, "Will you preach next Sunday?" I'm a twenty-year-old youth pastor with no training in how to study the Bible, let alone write a sermon. So, I take out a notebook and write what I know other preachers have done. I remember a sermon from when I was twelve years old where the preacher used Superman as an illustration for Christ. That hit hard, but I can't redo Superman, that would be a direct rip-off, so I'll do Spiderman. We are knee-deep in that first Sam Raimi film trilogy—perfect. But Spiderman is not Superman. He's not really an allegory for Jesus. So, what can I say about Spiderman? Well, Uncle Ben did say, "With great power comes great responsibility." That's it! A sermon about understanding our great responsibility with the Gospel. But what Bible verse goes with that? Well, the Great Commission works, but everyone does that text. I could do

Tony's Life Tip

Spiderman 2 is one of the best comic book movies. Revisit it.

What is a Sermon?

something in Acts; that book has a lot of stuff going on. Should I go ahead and just read the book? No, that seems like a lot of work. I think I heard someone preach on Phillip. I think he disappeared at some point and brought the Gospel to an Egyptian person. That sounds miracle-y enough to make the leap to Spiderman. Phillip knew he had to use the great responsibility of the Gospel to reach the lost. Perfect. Now, what should I do with the other 20 minutes of the sermon?

I wish this story weren't true. I wish that I could say that I had a deep respect for hermeneutics and a strong homiletic when I first started preaching. But through my own sanctification path, I've learned that I should not lie. The truth is, I was young, dumb, and thought I could preach sermons just because I liked being in front of people. My natural charisma would carry it all. I wrote that sermon and preached that sermon. I went up there, and before 100 people talked about Spiderman and Phillip, repeated myself about 200 times, and nervously laughed my way through 12 minutes of a sermon. My pastor, dear friend, and mentor, Aaron Norwood, told me after, "Well, I don't think you were ready for that." I wasn't. I didn't know how to read the Bible, let alone preach it well.

Aaron didn't allow me to stay that way. He forced me to take a hermeneutics class and worked with me on preparing a simple homiletic. Over the next years, he gave me opportunities to preach. He allowed me to be the sole preacher of the newly established 8:30 am service, and those 35 people suffered through some rough sermons. And then, when I was ready, he retired and handed the church over to me. Aaron walked me step-by-step through how to preach well, gave me opportunities, and then allowed me to lead.

Pastoral Tip

We need to get the next generation of preachers ready. That means we train, give opportunities, and give honest feedback.

What is a Sermon?

He allowed me to fail and then corrected me. I will forever be grateful for his influence on my life.

And now, after 20 years of ministry, God has moved my life into training the next generation of pastors, to be what Aaron was to me.

CHAPTER 3

A Three-Day Plan

A common and well-used phrase is that if you fail to plan, then you plan to fail. In order to make this process work, you have to plan well and be dedicated to the plan. This plan is to write a sermon in three days. On average, the process will take six to eight hours. Many of you reading that just gave me a hard stop. "I don't think or write that way." Or "My church calendar is too packed or unpredictable to do this." Let me be honest. It's not. This is a simple discipline. Here's a brief overview that I hope will encourage you.

Monday: Sermon Prep, Research, Big Idea
Tuesday: Sermon Outline and Applications
Wednesday: Sermon Intro, Outro, Illustrations

Pastoral Tip

You have to strike a balance between pastoral duties and sermon prep. Some weeks you may have to give more time to either one. So be prepared.

A Three-Day Plan

Each one of these days takes anywhere between one-and a- half to three hours, depending on the text and how far you are in your series. I use the time between 8:00 and 10:00 a.m. to work this process. Why? Because I drop off my kids at 7:30, our meetings at church normally don't start until 10:30, and I'm most awake between those hours. That might not be you. One of our staff members works best between the hours of 10:00 p.m. and midnight. This is when I would recommend he work the process. The timing is up to you, but you have to be dedicated to completing the work. Give your best time to God. I would recommend finding your most aware and awake times and dedicating that time to the process. It will take commitment. It will take saying no. But if you follow the process, you will find that you actually have more time for other ministry activities.

I didn't always use a three-day model. I used to stretch it out over four days, but then COVID hit in 2020. Some of you are recoiling while remembering that time. I was a pastor in California when we shut down and had to video every sermon. We would record on Thursdays, so I had to shorten the four-day process to three. What I found is that I worked better under the three-day timeline. I had a church with between 200-300 members. That meant my staff was not big enough to cover all the responsibilities, so I had to do a lot. I was at the hospital. I was at the Bible studies. I was taking the trash out. And even with everything that comes with pastoring a small to mid-size church, ninety-five percent of the time, I could work this three-day process.

I am a slow learner. You might not be. I need someone to work the process and actually walk me through it in order for me

Pastoral Tip

As of 2021, 65% of churches average less than 100 people.

https://research.lifeway.com/2021/10/20/small-churches-continue-growing-but-in-number-not-size/

A Three-Day Plan

to learn it. You are probably a lot smarter than me but indulge me. As I teach the process, I am going to work the process using 2 Timothy 3:16.

MONDAY
Day One

CHAPTER 4

Starting Your Day

Monday Morning Scenario One

The alarm hits. The first thing you think is, "I shouldn't have said that yesterday." You go downstairs and get your morning coffee. You attempt to read your morning devotion, but you can't stop thinking of all the other preachers who did a better job with that text. You question your call. You question your life choices. You think about that one dude in the church who was mean-mugging you. "He's probably not even saved," you think. You ask your wife, "Hey, do you think that sermon was ok?" Your wife responds in kindness and snark, "Will you believe me this time?" Your energy is spent. You are tired. This is why you take Mondays off.

Monday Morning Scenario Two

You wake up. You think about how blessed your people are that they got to hear that message. It was a banger. You can't believe that a revival didn't break out on the spot. You check your phone and there are no texts about how great the sermon was, but they're coming. You are sure of it. You walk downstairs and get your morning coffee. You start your devotion, but you are preoccupied. By what? By next week's killer sermon you are writing. Your people are so blessed. Not every church has a young Chuck Spurgeon.

Monday Morning Scenario Three

You wake up. You go downstairs to get your morning coffee. You read your devotion. Kiss your wife goodbye. Go to the office, break out the laptop, and ask yourself, "What did I preach yesterday?"

While each of these scenarios is a slight exaggeration of what a preacher feels on a Monday, all preachers can relate to them. You might be only one, or you could be an amalgamation of all three, but you can relate. I personally am scenario three. I have a short memory. God has blessed me with the ability to forget bad sermons, but trust me, I have plenty of them. I have the moments when I step down from the pulpit and I look into my loving wife's eyes and see the words that she is not going to say: "That wasn't great."

If you are Scenario One, you live in the sermon hangover. That's a struggle. You might not ever get over that. So, your Monday might be your Tuesday, but don't let it get farther than that. If you are Scenario Two, get people in your life to speak the truth. Get someone to critique your sermons often. But also, you need to focus. Forget yesterday and push it to next week. For Scenario Three people like me, it is important to review your past

Starting Your Day

notes and sermons. Make sure the text and applications are still on your heart. But whichever scenario is you, understand that Sunday is coming, and it's time to get to work.

The goal of this chapter is easy: to show you how to get through your first day of prep. This is your most important day—the day in which you build and understand the foundation of the sermon. The biblical text will hit your heart, head, and hands. At the end of this day's session, you will have a Big Idea of the text, an applicational outline, an argument for why both are accurate, all of your resources checked, and answers to ten of the most important questions for your sermon. You will be working through the Preaching Preparation Document, found at the end of the book. After today, you will not need any other documents to finish the week. Get ready! Monday is my favorite day of the week!

CHAPTER 5

Pray and Meditate on the Word

Every preaching book has the "pray" section at the beginning of their prep time. Why? Because without prayer and meditation on the word, our prep is only a process and not an intimate time with God. This is more than the "Jesus," "Bible," and "Pray" sections. Preaching is not just about the head. It is about the heart. We are taking the breathed-out Word of God and bringing it to His people. There are very few things as sacred. So you need to pray and meditate on the Word.

We don't need a justification for why we should pray and meditate on the Word, but let's give one anyway. 2 Timothy 3:16 provides ample reason why the Word of God is important. But I have a heart problem. I tend to shy away from the emotion of God's Word. Note that while we start with prayer and meditation on the Word right now, this will continue throughout the week.

Some pastors can accomplish this easily, but some struggle. I struggle. I need help focusing and getting lost in God's powerful

Word. At the end of the book, I've included two resources to help you get in the right space to pray and meditate on God's Word. The first is a collection of verses from Psalm 119. I'm going to give you a moment of vulnerability: I struggle with the Psalms. I tend to get impatient and want to move on to the more doctrinal aspects of Scripture. That struggle easily moves into my sermon prep. This prayer and meditation on the Word are vital to my spiritual health and to my preaching. The longest Psalm in the Bible is dedicated to the Word of God, and it is beautifully emotional. Read through the Psalm and meditate on the importance of meditating on God's Word. Slow down. Read these verses. Thank God for them.

The second resource is a copy of the daily morning liturgy from the 2019 Anglican *Book of Prayer*. (Hey, stop it! I'm very much Baptist, but this is a great resource.) As I said before, I struggle with meditation. You might, too. If you don't, feel free to skip this section. But if you do, I encourage you to work through a traditional liturgy. I work through this liturgy every day while kneeling on my prayer bench. It is not for tradition's sake that I do this. Instead, this simple liturgy helps me to meditate on the text and focus my mind on our Savior as I prepare to write a sermon. I've modified and added to this daily liturgy the text that we will be studying.

 **Timing:** 20-30 Minutes

CHAPTER 6

Verse Diagram

lright, we are prayed and meditated up, let's start ripping into the text. I always start with a verse diagram.

STOP: A Quick Warning

Often, when preachers begin to prep, the first thing they do is take out a commentary. STOP RIGHT NOW! STOP! DO NOT DO THAT. You are not preaching someone else's ideas on the text. You need to form your own. We will get to commentaries, but only after you have a strong grip on the text. Commentaries should validate your positions and outlines, not build them for you.

Back to the diagram. You will find that our study methodology follows a grammatical/historical/theological hermeneutic. This means that we start by studying what the actual words are saying. Then, we place them in the context of the original hearer. Finally, we study them throughout the Bible's story. If you need a brush-up in hermeneutics, I encourage you to buy Duvall and Hays's *Grasping God's Word*.

A verse diagram is a simple way of focusing on the words on the page. The goal is to get away from a wealth of knowledge, bias, and past learnings that you have and focus on the actual words. Many great pastors and theologians work through this process in much more depth than I do. A verse diagram will take verses and break them into natural sections of language. But the reality is, I'm not great at grammar. I have trouble remembering what an adverb is. So, I found a simple way to verse-diagram that works within my strengths and that I believe achieves much of the same result. Here are the two verses in 2 Timothy:

> **16** *All Scripture is breathed out by God and profitable for teaching, for reproof, for correction, and for training in righteousness,* **17** *that the man of God may be complete, equipped for every good work.*

Verse Diagram

Now let's break them down:

All Scripture
    Is breathed out by God
    And profitable for:
        Teaching
        Reproof
        Correction
        And for training in righteousness
    That the man of God
        May be
            Complete
            Equipped for every good work

That is a simple breakdown, but why break it down like this? Here is why:

All Scripture
the subject of the verses

> *Is breathed out by God*
> attribute of the subject
>
> *And profitable for:*
> application of the subject
>
>> *Teaching*
>> why it is profitable
>>
>> *Reproof*
>> why it is profitable
>>
>> *Correction*
>> why it is profitable
>>
>> *And for training in righteousness*
>> why it is profitable

That the man of God
the second subject that is affected by the first.

> *May be*
>
>> *Complete*
>> actions of the first subject on the second subject
>>
>> *Equipped for every good work*
>> actions of the first subject on the second subject

Verse Diagram

After the diagram is done, I print it out and start writing on it by hand. Writing on it creates an intimacy with the text. There is no wrong way to do this. Write what you see, what it says, possible rhythms, repeated words, and maybe even a few big ideas. Get familiar with the text.

After you have diagrammed the verse and scribbled all over the diagram, keep that paper out because you will refer to it often. As we move on to the exegetical outline, our main source will be this verse diagram.

 **Timing:** 20 Minutes

CHAPTER 7

Exegetical Outline

A little over a year ago, my family made the move to the American Midwest. We've always lived in the west. I was born in San Diego, California, lived most of my life in Arizona, and served as a senior pastor in Napa, California. My definition of "cold" was anything below fifty degrees. As I type this, I'm looking out my window and snow is on the ground. We just had a week of near zero-degree weather. I have a new definition of cold. Interestingly, if my current self went to visit my two-years-ago self, we would have different definitions of the same word. Only two years and with the same person. How significant would 2,000 years be, with a different government and ethnicity? That is why we start with the exegetical outline before we write our applicational outline.

A Quick Hermeneutical Detour

Before we get to the exegetical outline, we need to talk about the process of interpretation. If you're a pastor reading this book, I expect you to know what I'm about to say. Sadly, I didn't know this when I first started preaching. That is why my sermons were about superheroes and not Jesus. To prepare an exegetical outline, you must believe that there is only one correct interpretation of any area of the Bible. That interpretation is the intended message from the original writer, The Holy Spirit and person He used to write to the intended audience. If you do not believe this, then you cannot complete this section, and you have a major issue in your theology of the Bible. So, fix that and come back to work this chapter.

What is an exegetical outline? An exegetical outline is used to come to an understanding of what the text would have said to the people who originally heard it. It is the closest you can get to the correct interpretation of the text. In order to understand and write the exegetical outline, you need to do some contextual work. When I say contextual work, I still do not mean moving to commentaries yet. This work can easily be done with a simple Study Bible. You just need to know the who, when, why, and where of the passage. This will be most important when you are starting a new series in a new book. You have to get really comfortable knowing that information right off the top of your head. Let's answer the questions for 2 Timothy. For this, I will be using the ESV Study Bible:

- Who: Paul the Apostle is writing to Timothy, a pastor and elder of Ephesus.
- When: Paul's second letter, written around 66 AD.
- Why: Paul is telling Timothy to remain faithful to the Gospel, good doctrine, and the Bible. False teaching is entering the church.

Exegetical Outline

- Where: Paul is in Prison in Rome. Timothy is most likely in Ephesus.

Alright, the work is not done. In fact, this is not the exegetical outline. It is just the background for the exegetical outline. Now, we get to the outline. We start with the Big Idea the author is trying to convey.

1. Big Idea: Paul is telling Timothy that the Bible is God's Word and changes the life of the believer.

It's a little wordy, but that's ok for the exegetical outline. We'll clean that up when we get to the applicational outline. Next, we move to the subpoints that either apply the Big Idea or continue the argument for the Big Idea:

2. Big Idea: Paul is telling Timothy that the Bible is God's Word and changes the life of the believer.

- **Subpoint 1:** The Bible is "breathed out" by God.
- **Subpoint 2:** The Bible is good for teaching.
- **Subpoint 3:** The Bible is good for reproof.
- **Subpoint 4:** The Bible is good for correction.
- **Subpoint 5:** The Bible is good for training in righteousness.
- **Subpoint 6:** The Bible makes the man complete.
- **Subpoint 7:** The Bible makes us equipped to do good works.

I know, this is literally the verse diagram repeated. But this process helps us move to an applicational sermon. We start seeing and hearing what the original audience would have heard. This is the simple process of the exegetical outline. Do not skip it! Now, onto the applicational outline, the outline of what we are going to preach.

Timing: 15 Minutes

CHAPTER 8

Applicational Outline

A good friend and fantastic pastor, Adam Bailie, once told a group that I was a part of, "The purpose of a sermon is a high view of God, and the purpose of preaching is life change." Many preachers stop at the first. They are faithful to write a sermon that makes much of the text to the original audience and then forget they have to preach it to *their church*. The move to their congregation is clunky at best. And so we have a ton of people with some knowledge about the Greek word for any given verse and no place or no ability to use it. The preacher forgets to make the last transition in hermeneutics to the audience of today. If the purpose of preaching is a life change, then we must make the sermon applicable. We have to tell our people what to do with the text they've just heard explained. This is the process of converting an exegetical outline to an applicational outline.

Exegetical to Applicational

Let's take a look at our exegetical outline again:

3. Big Idea: Paul is telling Timothy that the Bible is God's Word and changes the life of the believer.

- **Subpoint 1:** The Bible is "breathed out" by God.
- **Subpoint 2:** The Bible is good for teaching.
- **Subpoint 3:** The Bible is good for reproof.
- **Subpoint 4:** The Bible is good for correction.
- **Subpoint 5:** The Bible is good for training in righteousness.
- **Subpoint 6:** The Bible makes the man complete.
- **Subpoint 7:** The Bible makes us equipped to do good works.

We need to start with the Big Idea. We need to change the Exegetical Big Idea to an Applicational Big Idea or the Big Idea of the sermon. Duvall and Hays, in the book *Grasping God's Word*, would call this the "timeless theological principle." They present the following rules to this principle, which I changed to Big Idea for consistency in this book:

1. The Big Idea should be reflected in the text.
2. The Big Idea should be timeless and not tied to a specific situation.
3. The Big Idea should not be culturally bound.
4. The Big Idea should correspond to the teaching of the rest of Scripture.
5. The Big Idea should be relevant to both the biblical and the contemporary audience.

Applicational Outline

Although not part of their book, I'm going to add two more:

6. The Big Idea should be directed to your audience/church
7. The Big Idea should be less than 12 words.

Speak to the congregation. We know they're there. Look at them and tell them what they need to know. Keep it quick and simple. Let's try this with 2 Timothy:

> 4. **Exegetical Big Idea:** Paul is telling Timothy that the Bible is God's Word and changes the life of the believer.
>
> 5. **Applicational Big Idea (first draft):** The Bible is God's Word and will change you.

A few things I like about this Big Idea are that it's true and doesn't break our rules, and it speaks directly to the listener. What I don't like about this Big Idea is that it's clunky and not memorable. Let's try again:

Applicational Big Idea (first draft):
The Bible is God's Word and will change you.

Applicational Big Idea (second draft):
God's Word transforms us.

I like it, but instantly I notice that I'm going to have to do some due diligence to ensure that people know that God's Word is spoken out by Him, but I think we can explain that idea in more detail in the subpoints. So, let's move to the subpoints.

When working through your subpoints you need to relate them back to the Big Idea or else you run the threat of preaching multiple Big Ideas. If that is the case, you may have taken too big a chunk of Scripture, and you need to split the sermon into two. So how do we avoid preaching multiple Big Ideas? We ask a question pertaining to the Big Idea that the subpoints will answer. For this sermon on 2 Timothy 3:16,17, let's settle on this question:

6. Question for the Big Idea: How does God's Word transform us?

Let's use the text to create the subpoints. The first thing I notice about our exegetical subpoints is that there are seven. People cannot remember seven subpoints, even when they write them down. Let's make it simpler. But how? Well, looking at the subpoints, we find some consistencies that could be grouped together. Subpoint 1, The Bible is "breathed out" by God, needs to stand on its own. Let's use that subpoint to answer the question.

- **Exegetical Subpoint 1:** The Bible is "breathed out" by God.
- **Applicational Subpoint 1:** We have access to God's literal words.

The subpoint answers the question and also moves the concept of "breathed-out" into a more modern language that our people can understand. Now let's bring some of these Subpoints together. Subpoints two through five can be consolidated because they have a common theme. Let's do this:

- **Exegetical Subpoint 2:** The Bible is good for teaching.
- **Exegetical Subpoint 3:** The Bible is good for reproof.
- **Exegetical Subpoint 4:** The Bible is good for correction.

Applicational Outline

- **Exegetical Subpoint 5:** The Bible is good for training in righteousness.
- **Applicational Subpoint 2:** God's Word guides us to be different.

I like this point. The idea of a guide puts the onus on us to follow God's Word. Notice that I reused the Big Idea phrase of God's Word. It didn't fit our first subpoint, but that's okay, the phrase is down first here. Alright let's finish it out by consolidating the last two. Why? Because they form a natural cut-point in the verse and bridge the transition to verse 17, which introduces the concept of "completion," which will be difficult to break down.

- **Exegetical Subpoint 6:** The Bible makes the man complete.
- **Exegetical Subpoint 7:** The Bible makes us equipped to do good works.
- **Applicational Subpoint 3:** God's Word leads us to live as God intended.

Alright, there we go. This allows us to go into greater detail about "completeness" while also showing that our works demonstrate our salvation and position in the kingdom. So, let's put it all together. Here is our applicational outline - what people will see and hear from the pulpit:

7. Applicational Big Idea (second draft): God's Word transforms us.

8. **Question for the Big Idea: How does God's Word transform us?**

- **Applicational Subpoint 1:** We have access to God's literal words.
- **Applicational Subpoint 2:** God's Word guides us to be different.
- **Applicational Subpoint 3:** God's Word leads us to live as God intended.

Alright, the outline is done. This will be your longest process of day one. Now, the moment you have all been waiting for, it's time to hit those commentaries.

 **Timing:** 30 Minutes

CHAPTER 9

Resources

Agatha's Poirot

Two years ago, my wife and I started reading Agatha Christie's Poirot novels. Agatha Christie was a prolific writer who wrote scores of novels during a career spanning from the early 1900s into the 1970s. Most of her works are detective or mystery novels. Possibly her most famous book was Murder on the Orient Express. We were looking for something to do as a couple and decided we would each get a copy and read them together. Then through the week, we would sit and talk about who we thought the murderer was.

We are roughly twenty books in now. It is sweet, and I look forward to the time together. But there is one problem: we are both highly competitive. We started racing each other to the finish and to the major reveal. With that in mind, there is one major temptation: to look at the back of the book. To cheat the system. To win by all means. While the temptation is strong, we have never done it (yet). Why? Because the point of the activity is to be with each other, to discover the book together. If we cheat the system, we are working against the reason we are doing this in the first place. In the same way, sermon prep is not about racing to the end of the outline. Sermons are about discovering! Discovering is not about regurgitating someone else's ideas and research. We have to get there on our own. That is why we do minimal work on resources until this point of the process. If you've worked the prep as laid out, you have:

- Prayed and meditated on the Word
- Diagrammed the verse
- Created an Exegetical Outline
- Moved it to an Application Outline

You know the text! You have done the work. Now, when we get to resources, our goals have shifted.

A quick aside: I am currently working through a series in Genesis. I am not an expert in Genesis. As I start this series, I am doing a lot of research with resources before I verse diagram. While this is not the norm, I need to make sure I'm adequately prepared for a weak area in my biblical training. There will be times when you need to do this and break from routine.

The goal of using resources is to verify your work and gather new information from experts you would otherwise not have access to. It is not about taking their ideas and declaring them yours. Commentaries, maps, dictionaries, and the like should be used to build out your sermon, not write it for you.

Which sources should you use? Well, different texts and

Resources

genres will require different sources. But for any given text, I would encourage the use of the following resources:

- An exegetical commentary
- A lexicon resource
- A devotional commentary

There could be unique resources or books written about the exact text you are preaching that you might take into consideration also. The first goal of these resources is to verify the work that you've done. If you are far off what they say, you may have made a wrong turn and need to be corrected. While this does not happen often, it will happen from time to time. The second goal of using resources is to gather new information that you could not have known. There are many scholars who are smarter than me and have researched much more than I have. Stand on their shoulders, but do not steal their work. Give them credit if you use their research.

A quick warning: this is the point where we all need to acknowledge an insecurity. We all want to appear smart. As a preacher, you have the unique opportunity weekly to prove how smart you are. STOP IT! That is pride and sinful. Throw that temptation away. You have to keep your people in mind when using resources. They do not want to hear you try to pronounce every Greek word or quote fifteen scholars in every sermon. *Preach to your people.* Take what you need from these resources and move on!

Timing: 30-45 Minutes

CHAPTER 10

Answer the Questions

I am a child of the 80s and 90s, meaning I don't know how to build or operate anything. So it was appropriate that at age 17, I got a job at Ace Hardware. They put me in the nuts-and-bolts section. I barely knew what either of them were. So, I faked it. People would come in and ask for a certain size bolt, and then I would point to an area and say, "I believe they're in that section." Then I would go get Steve, the sixty-year-old retired construction worker, to answer the question. Two things about Steve: he was always kinda drunk, and he knew where the bolt was. He could point to where the bolts were with his eyes closed.

Too many preachers write sermons on text they barely know. Monday is a day to ensure that we know the text. We should be able to answer questions about the verse, context, and Big Idea without blinking.

Let's wrap up Monday. You made it! It's close to the end of the first day. Now, all you have to do is verify that you actually know what you're talking about. On the front of the Preaching Preparation Document there are ten questions we have been avoiding until now. Now is the time to answer the questions. The goal is to answer them without having to look up any new information. If you can do that, you are ready for Tuesday. Here are the ten questions:

1. **What's the Big Idea?**
2. **Tweet the point: (180 characters or less)**
   This is the one that most people struggle with. The idea is that we can succinctly state the sermon in a way that catches the listener.
3. **What do you want them to know?**
4. **What do you want them to feel?**
5. **What do you want them to do?**
6. **What is the context?**
7. **What would people lose if this text weren't there?**
8. **How does this connect to the Gospel?**
9. **Big Idea Question we are answering:**
10. **What are the subpoints?**

Each of these questions should be answered in less than three sentences. The questions are pretty obvious, but let's answer them for 2 Timothy 3:16,17:

1. **What's the Big Idea?**
   God's Word transforms us.
2. **Tweet the point: (180 characters or less)**
   God has spoken and had it written down for us, why waste it?

Answer the Questions

3. **What do you want them to know?**
   The Bible is literally God's Word and can transform our lives.
4. **What do you want them to feel?**
   An appreciation for God's Word and a desire to read and follow it.
5. **What do you want them to do?**
   Create a daily reading plan. Note: This is the first time we address application. Take this time to develop a simple and direct application that the congregation can make that week.
6. **What is the context?**
   Paul is writing to Timothy, a young pastor of the church at Ephesus, about how to keep the church doctrinally sound.
7. **What would people lose if this text weren't there?**
   The significance of God's Word and the life change it brings.
8. **How does this connect to the Gospel?**
   God's Word is the story of redemption. It points us to salvation through Christ and then the process of sanctification.
9. **Big Idea Question we are answering:**
   How does God's Word transform us?
10. **What are the subpoints?**
    - We have access to God's literal words.
    - God's Word guides us to be different.
    - God's Word leads us to live as God intended.

Simple Sermons

Alright, questions answered! Our Monday is done! Now, we can take the rest of the day to do all the other ministry stuff we are charged with. Great job!

 Timing: 5 Minutes

Total timing for the day:
2 hours 25 minutes

TUESDAY
Day Two

CHAPTER 11

The Holy Spirit and the Sermon Writer

At seventeen years old, I walked into my first Southern Baptist Church. For the most part, my high school years were far from God. So I needed church — really, I needed Jesus. I found the biggest church in my little town, which was, and still is, a Southern Baptist Church, and went. From that moment on, for better or for worse, I've been a Southern Baptist. There is plenty to love about the Baptist traditions, but there can be difficulties. One area of difficulty is the complex relationship that Baptists, particularly Southern Baptists, have with the Holy Spirit. From my experience, it seems we don't really know how to engage with the third part of the Trinity. I especially felt that myself until I started writing sermons every week.

There is nothing that engages me more with the Holy Spirit than the process of filling out my sermon outline. At the back of the book, I've provided a Sermon Outline document. I recommend you use it. But understand that the document does not write the sermon for you. It's you, the Word of God, and the Holy Spirit guiding you to write a sermon that speaks to your people. It is special. The process is sacred. It is worship. And if you think of it any less, you are demeaning the wonderful responsibility of writing and preaching sermons.

You know the text. You've done your research, and now you are prepared to write. If you allow the Spirit to move in this time, you will find that you can intimately explain and apply the text to the congregation that God has blessed you to pastor. The relationship that is formed between you and the people that God has given you to temporally oversee will bear fruit in power, conviction, and clarity in the sermon writing process. It is the time when I can get the closest to being charismatic. I approach the sermon with anxiety, and then I start typing, and it comes alive. God knows what the people need to hear from the text. It is special and powerful. This is our Tuesday. This is our Day Two. Let's have some fun and start filling out this sermon.

CHAPTER 12

Sermon Outline

I think linearly. I can't help it. When things are not clear, or if A does not explicitly point to B, I get frustrated. To alleviate these frustrations, I push structure and routines. That is why I write my sermons in three days. I wake up at the same time every day, 6:15. I have the same morning routine: check my phone, take a shower, go downstairs. I read the Bible in the same chair. I drink the same amount of coffee each day, four cups. I eat the same breakfast every day, one slice of peanut butter toast. So, of course, I use the same sermon outline every week. But as I stated before, this is the Toyota Corolla of homiletics. This sermon outline has rarely let me down. Let's review the outline:

Simple Sermons

Sermon Outline Document

Series:	
Text:	
Sermon Date:	
Big Idea:	
Intro	
Reading	
The case for the Big Idea	
Question for the Big Idea	
Subpoint 1	
Explanation	
Illustration	
Application	
Subpoint 2	
Explanation	
Illustration	
Application	
Subpoint 3	
Explanation	
Illustration	
Application	
Next Steps	
Outro	
Prayer	

Sermon Outline

Ok, there is the outline. Pretty basic. Let's walk through the parts and in the next section I will show how to organize the work we've already done. The first section is easy enough. I've learned that my sermon outline should start with the basic information like series title and text. This will help us organize our sermons later on in life, for when you want to torture yourself by looking at older sermons. Next is a clear statement of the Big Idea. We will not say it upfront, but it is the heart and focus of the sermon. Now, we are getting into the actual sermon outline. The sermon needs to grab the heart of the listener. An illustration in the intro typically does this, but we don't need to worry about that until tomorrow, Wednesday. The Reading is the actual reading of the text you are studying. In our church, we have the people stand for this reading. You don't need to make them stand, but you do need to read it to them.

Next is The Case for the Big Idea. In this section, we will argue why the Big Idea is essential for their lives. I include the bulk of the contextual work in this section. The following section is the body of the sermon. I always include the question for the Big Idea to keep me on track. All the subpoints include an explanation, illustration, and application. After the subpoints, we give them two to three next steps. These are practical and specific applications for the week. Finish the sermon with the outro, the emotional appeal related to the intro. I always include specific items I will use in my prayer.

Well, that was a lot. I get it. I'm not going to leave you here. Over the next sections, we are going to go into more detail on each area while filling out the Sermon Outline. A quick note on the Sermon Outline: this is a guide not a law. Every sermon is

Simple Sermons

going to look a little different. I've preached sermons with four subpoints and other sermons with just one. I'll have an illustration for each subpoint, or I'll skip one or two. Do not become legalistic with the Sermon Outline. It is here to serve you; you do not have to serve it. Remember, writing a sermon is a holy activity. It is worship. Do not let it become mechanical. Take time and allow the Holy Spirit to navigate you through the process. You know the text. So that was Monday. Now have some fun.

CHAPTER 13

Organize

I've already confessed my need for routine. Now, I need to confess my need for order. I like it when things are in a nice and neat order. I am the guy who cooks dinner, washes the dishes, sets up the table, and takes the first bite after everything is in order, even when I'm eating alone. Before we get into writing the sermon, we need to take the information we already have from the preaching preparation document and put it into our sermon outline document. Let's do that with 2 Timothy 3:16,17.

Series:	Faithful Church
Text:	2 Timothy 3:16,17
Sermon Date:	1/01/2075
Big Idea:	God's Word transforms us.
Intro	

Reading	***2 Timothy 3:16,17*** **16** *All Scripture is breathed out by God and profitable for teaching, for reproof, for correction, and for training in righteousness,* **17** *that the man of God may be complete, equipped for every good work.* **Pastor:** This is the Word of the Lord **All:** Thanks be to God
The case for the Big Idea	
Question for the Big Idea	How does God's Word transform us?
Subpoint 1	We have access to God's literal words. **16** *All Scripture is breathed out by God . .*
Explanation	
Illustration	
Application	
Subpoint 2	God's Word guides us to be different. *and profitable for teaching, for reproof, for correction, and for training in righteousness . . .*
Explanation	
Illustration	
Application	
Subpoint 3	God's Word leads us to live as God intended. **17** *that the man of God may be complete, equipped for every good work.*
Explanation	

Organize

Illustration	
Application	
Next Steps	
Outro	
Prayer	

I know that you're asking, "Did you just copy and paste all of this?" The answer is yes, I did. But this process shows our sermon's backbone. It brings clarity to what we are about to say, and it's more important than it seems. Most of the parts are pretty self-explanatory. One key area I would like to highlight is the text under the subpoints. It is important to put that text there so that you can verify it fits the subpoint and stays anchored to the Word. The next section is building out the Case for the Big Idea.

 Timing: Less than 5 Minutes

CHAPTER 14

The Case for the Big Idea

When my kids were young, I could tell them anything and they would just believe it. Like many young kids, they loved animals. They especially loved the show *Wild Kratts*. It is a PBS show where two brothers explore animal life. They start in the real world by showing an animal and then cut to a cartoon world, where they both magically look a lot younger, and where they tell a story with the animals. The show was on repeat in my house.

One weekend, we took our kids up to northern Arizona to go camping. As we were driving, my seven-year-old son asked about the difference between brown bears and grizzly bears. I answered, "Well, son, all brown bears *are* grizzly bears. They are the same." To which he replied, "No, you're wrong." I promptly punished him for questioning his father and asking a question he already knew the answer to. Okay, I didn't do that, but I did double down. "Yes, son, they are." "No, Dad, all grizzly bears are brown bears, but not all brown bears are grizzly bears." To which my wife said, after looking it up on her phone, "He's right." I learned two things that day. 1. No more *Wild Kratts*; they were undermining my authority. 2. My kids were not just going to take my word for it any longer.

Many pastors I work with assume their church is just going to listen to them. They do not need to develop an argument with good research. Their sermons do not need to present a solid case for their Big Idea. We are discounting our people when we think like this. Like in any good public address, we need to present an argument and explain why it is important for the listener. This section of the sermon is called The Case for the Big Idea. It comes right after the opening illustration, and it introduces the text while setting up the reason the congregation needs this applicational sermon in their life.

The goal of this section is to give the context of the passage and transport it to now. It is the mini-hermeneutic for the sermon. The goal is to form an argument that demonstrates the need for the change the text calls for. There should be a hard charge at the hoop during this section. It's not just a historical presentation, it's preaching. There is power in the context and power in the current call on our life. Let's write out the case for the Big Idea for 2 Timothy 3:16,17.

A quick note on the sermon going forward. I do not write a manuscript for my sermons. I use an in-depth outline I write in my cadence and rhythm of speech. It uses short phrases that only I understand. I randomly capitalize stuff I want to emphasize. It is a mess. In fact, the pastor I currently serve under stated, "I have no idea how to preach from this." It would help no one if I used that here, so I'm not going to. Instead, I am going to develop the sections in manuscript form, with a few outlines to demonstrate the beginning phases. The sermon length I'm going for in this book is about twenty minutes. I typically preach around thirty, so I took a third off for brevity's sake. Alright, now let's get back to that Case for the Big Idea.

What do we need?

We start this process by laying out the facts that we need for this section. Most likely, we do not need as much as you think we do. We do not need every textual theory or variance of words. Just give them everything they need to understand the passage and the Big Idea. The best place to look is at the answers to the questions on the Preaching Preparation Document. For our sermon, we need the following:

1. **What's the Big Idea?**
   God's Word transforms us.
2. **Tweet the point:**
   God has spoken and had it written down for us, why waste it?
3. **What is the context?**
   Paul is writing to Timothy, a young pastor of the church at Ephesus, about how to keep the church doctrinally sound.
4. **What would people lose if this text weren't there?**
   The significance of God's Word and the life change it brings.

5. **Big Idea Question we are answering:**
How does God's Word transform us?

The other questions will be used in our subpoints and outro. For this section, these questions will suffice. But just listing the questions does not build the case. You need to form your rhetoric. Rhetoric may seem like a bad word, but it's not. We're not talking about emotional manipulation; we're preaching to our people at the level at which they think and feel.

- Logos: logic and reason
- Pathos: emotion
- Ethos: character

This is the way we process and remember information. It's okay to speak to the attributes. Let's try it out with 2 Timothy.

The Case for our Big Idea: God's Word transforms us.

There is one constant in this world, it is change. We are not created to be stagnant. Our bodies change. Our personalities change. Our beliefs change. Even as followers of Jesus, our theology changes and matures. However, there is definitely change that is not good. And you have a choice on what will ultimately transform you.

This question was one of the largest issues in the early church. A man named Paul went throughout the Middle East, Europe, and parts of Asia, preached the Gospel, and started churches. One of his favorite churches is in a city named Ephesus. Ephesus was a major trade and religious center in Rome. Ephesus had a large temple dedicated to Artemus, the Roman Goddess. It was

The Case for the Big Idea

one of the seven wonders of the ancient world. People would come from all over to worship there. And yet God used Paul to plant this church.

Paul loved this church. He sent his favorite pupil, Timothy, to pastor this church. He writes this church one of the most theologically significant letters, *Letter to the Ephesians*. Paul sets this church up to succeed the best he can, but the world does not stop its pursuit to transform us.

The church quickly came under attack by false doctrines. The Jews wanted the church to return to legalism. The Gnostics were speaking out against the divinity of Jesus. The Roman pagans were trying to push these new believers back to idol worship. The church was under attack. So Paul writes Timothy. He actually writes him twice. In the first letter he organizes the church. In this second letter, Paul's last letter, he is telling Pastor Timothy to protect the church from false doctrine. He doesn't want the church to be transformed by the world. He wants the world to be transformed by Christ's church.

How does Paul protect the church? He grounds its people in the only Word of God that we have. He tells them that the only godly transformation happens through the Holy Spirit speaking to them through the Word of God.

The truth is that the world is still trying to transform us. If you're a Christian, the world is constantly pulling you to your old nature. We still have false idols, false doctrines, and worldly passions that try to change us. But it is our choice of what we will allow to transform us. Will we go back to our old selves and live in the prison that Christ has freed us from? Or will he be transformed by His Holy Word?

God has spoken, why waste it? The Bible is not just a book that gives us good morals; it has the ability to transform us! So, what do you want to influence your life? Because God's Word *transforms us*. And today we will be answering: *How does God's Word transform us?*

Bible Study vs. Preaching

We made the argument. A couple of things I would like to point out. First, we could have gone into much more detail on any contextual item, but we didn't need to, at least not at this point. The goal was to give the people at the church at Ephesus what they needed to understand the passage. The way I teach the people I'm training is to ask a simple question: Is this Bible study material or preaching material?

When you teach a Bible study, you have a long time to answer questions, fill in gaps, and go much deeper. When you are preaching, you need to get to the point. You need to give them everything to understand and apply the passage. Most of the time, the extra stuff you want to say is just to make you sound more intelligent. It doesn't help the sermon. In fact, it could actually hurt the sermon. Ask yourself in this section what people need to know.

Drive it home.

The second thing I want to point out is that we need to drive that argument home. Make a plea. We want the people to think and feel that they *need* those applicational points from the text. Why? Because they need the applicational points for the text. If they didn't, there would be no use in preaching it. Call to them, drive it home.

After making the case for the Big Idea

Alright, the case is written. Let's update our sermon outline:

Series:	Faithful Church
Text:	2 Timothy 3:16,17
Sermon Date:	1/01/2075
Big Idea:	God's Word transforms us.
Intro	
Reading	*2 Timothy 3:16,17* *16 All Scripture is breathed out by God and profitable for teaching, for reproof, for correction, and for training in righteousness, 17 that the man of God may be complete, equipped for every good work.* **Pastor:** This is the Word of the Lord **All:** Thanks be to God
The case for the Big Idea	

There is one constant in this world. It is change. We are not created to be stagnant. Our bodies change. Our personalities change. Our beliefs change. Even as followers of Jesus, our theology changes and matures. However, there is definitely change that is not good. And you have a choice of what will ultimately transform you.

This question was one of the largest issues in the early church. A man named Paul went throughout the Middle East, Europe, and parts of Asia, preached the Gospel, and started churches. One of his favorite churches is in a city named Ephesus. Ephesus was a major trade and religious center in Rome. Ephesus had a large temple dedicated to Artemis, the Roman Goddess. It was one of the seven wonders of the ancient world. People would come from all over to worship there. And yet God used Paul to plant this church.

Paul loved this church, he sent his favorite pupil, Timothy, to pastor this church. He writes this church one of the most theologically significant letters, *Letter to the Ephesians*. Paul sets this church up to succeed the best he can, but the world does not stop its pursuit to transform us.

The church quickly came under attack by false doctrines. The Jews wanted the church to return to legalism. The Gnostics were speaking out against the divinity of Jesus. The Roman pagans were trying to push these new believers back to idol worship. The church was under attack. So, Paul writes Timothy. He actually writes him twice. In the first letter he organizes the church. In this second letter, Paul's last letter, he is telling Pastor Timothy to protect the church from false doctrine. He doesn't want the church to be transformed by the world. He wants the world to be transformed by Christ's church.

How does Paul protect the church? He grounds its people in the only Word of the God that we have. He tells them that the only godly transformation happens through the Holy Spirit speaking to them through the Word of God.

The Case for the Big Idea

The truth is that the world is still trying to transform us. If you're a Christian, the world is constantly pulling you to your old nature. We still have false idols, false doctrines, and worldly passions that try to change us. But it is our choice of what we will allow to transform us. Will we go back to our old selves and live in the prison that Christ has freed us from? Or will we be transformed by His Holy Word?

God has spoken, why waste it? The Bible is not just a book that gives us good morals; it has the ability to transform us! So, what do you want to influence your life? Because *God's Word transforms us.* Today, we will be answering the following questions: *How does God's Word transform us?*

Question for the Big Idea	How does God's Word transform us?
Subpoint 1	We have access to God's literal words. *16 All Scripture is breathed out by God . .*
Explanation	
Illustration	
Application	
Subpoint 2	God's Word guides us to be different. *and profitable for teaching, for reproof, for correction, and for training in righteousness . . .*
Explanation	
Illustration	
Application	

Subpoint 3	God's Word leads us to live as God intended. *17 that the man of God may be complete, equipped for every good work.*
Explanation	
Illustration	
Application	
Next Steps	
Outro	
Prayer	

 Timing: 30 Minutes

CHAPTER 15

Subpoints Explanation

We got their attention. What do we do next? Tell them how to apply the text in their lives. Give them the applicational subpoints. There will be two parts to these subpoints that we'll do in the next two sections of the book. First, we will write out the explanation, and then we will go to the application. I'm going to start by outlining the explanation, then I will write it in manuscript form. Let's start by taking a look at the three subpoints:

Question for the Big Idea: How does God's Word transform us?

Subpoint 1	We have access to God's literal words. *16 All Scripture is breathed out by God . .*
Explanation	
Illustration	
Application	

Subpoint 2	God's Word guides us to be different. *and profitable for teaching, for reproof, for correction, and for training in righteousness . . .*
Explanation	
Illustration	
Application	
Subpoint 3	God's Word leads us to live as God intended. *17 that the man of God may be complete, equipped for every good work.*
Explanation	.
Illustration	
Application	

For now, we will ignore the Illustration and Application sections. Let's outline the Explanation.

The outline is going to include all the relevant information we need the church to hear in order to get the subpoints, answer the question for the Big Idea, and get to the application. You need to think like your people. If you were explaining these ideas to them, what would they need to know? Remember these are normal people, not seminary people. People who wake up and take care of kids, go to jobs, probably pay mortgages, and watch TV at night. They might not be saved. They might have fought with their spouse this morning. Think like them. What do they need to grab these concepts? Each sermon and text are different. They'll need something different. This is where you pray for discernment and wisdom. This is where the Holy Spirit really

Subpoints Explanation

starts taking the wheel of this sermon. I'll present my outline and explain why below the outlined section.

Subpoint 1	We have access to God's literal words. *16 All Scripture is breathed out by God . .*

Explanation
What does "all Scripture" mean?
This is the entire Bible (affirmed in 2 Peter 1:20-21, amongst other places.)

What does "breathed out by God" mean?
- The words "breathed out" literally mean the expulsion of air in the lungs. Or, as I like to say, spoken.
- The Bible is spoken out by God.
    The Holy Spirit speaks to the human writers, and they write it down for the people.

If this is true, what are the implications?
- In the Bible, we can read the actual words of the Creator of the universe.
- The Bible has the authority of God!
- The Bible reveals God's Salvation.
- We cannot ignore it.

It feels basic, doesn't it? Explain the text and get to the implication. Readers, this isn't rocket science. God didn't call us to preach to show the world how smart we are. The best preachers take complete texts and make them simple for their people. Notice that I only included one proof text. There is a 50/50 chance that I will read it aloud. If I don't read it, I'll point people there to check out later. Most people do not need you to read every verse that pertains to every subject you hit. That is overwhelming. Also, notice that while I explain the "breathed out by God" line, I do not use Greek. I do not say the Greek. Don't be that person. No one wants to see you suffer through Greek pronunciation. Explain the word and move on. Lastly, I include implications but not applications. I want them to understand why this explanation is important, but the applications will come down the line. Let's move on to the second point.

Subpoint 2	God's Word guides us to be different. *and profitable for teaching, for reproof, for correction, and for training in righteousness* . . .

Explanation

Define Profitable: use a mini-illustration of an unprofitable venture.

Starting a lemonade stand doesn't make money.

What is the Bible profitable for?

Teaching: This is doctrine

- Define Doctrine: Doctrine is teachings of the Christian faith. It is what we believe.
- You will get doctrine either here or somewhere else.
- This is a major issue in the early churches.
    Sixteen of the twenty-seven books of the New Testament mention false teachers.

Subpoints Explanation

- This is a major issue now.

   The Bible is clear that people in the church will follow doctrines that are false.

   Reference: 2 Timothy 4:3-4

   Example: Prosperity Gospel

Reproof

Reproof is exposing error.

The Bible is all about reproof.

> ***Proverbs 12:1:*** *Whoever loves discipline loves knowledge, but he who hates reproof is stupid.*

Correction

Experiencing reproof without correction is a waste of time.

- We should want change.

Training in righteousness.

This is the goal of the Christian.

- We call this sanctification.

Hebrews 4:12

> *For the word of God is living and active, sharper than any two-edged sword, piercing to the division of soul and of spirit, of joints and of marrow, and discerning the thoughts and intentions of the heart.*

The Bible guides us to be different.

Transition: We have to want to be different.

This was a longer subpoint. You'll have those. The key is to understand the length and time you have in the sermon. We might cut some of this down on day three, but this all works for now.

In this section I included two proof-texts. Both of these verses will add to the application and make the sermon "punchier." The verses verify the information while adding something new to the sermon. Notice here that we just walk straight through the verse. This will help your people to understand how to pick apart the passage. While preaching the text, you're also training them how to read the Bible. The final thing I want you to see is the mini-illustration. A mini-illustration is a quick word picture that helps illuminate the quick point you are making. They should be less than thirty seconds. I do not use them often, but sometimes they are needed. Plus, we all know lemonade stands are a waste of time and money. Let's finish this outline.

Subpoint 3	God's Word leads us to live as God intended. *17 that the man of God may be complete, equipped for every good work.*

Explanation

Explain the brokenness of the world.
- We are not righteous.
- We are incomplete.

The Bible leads us to salvation.
- The story of redemption
- The Gospel
    Present the Gospel of the redemptive story of the Scripture:
    - The fall

Subpoints Explanation

- The Savior
- The death
- The resurrection and ascension
- The return

Romans 10:9,10

> *Because, if you confess with your mouth that Jesus is Lord and believe in your heart that God raised him from the dead, you will be saved. For with the heart one believes and is justified, and with the mouth one confesses and is saved.*

When we are saved, we are complete, but our completion is shown through our actions.

The Bible prepares us to be equipped for every good work.
- We live like God intended.
- We help heal the brokenness of the world.
- We bring the Gospel to the world.

This point can be summarized in two words: *The Gospel.* If you get nothing out of this book, please just listen to me right here: *If you do not have a clear Gospel presentation in every sermon, you have failed at your job.* You need to stop preaching. Every sermon is Christ-centered and should be wrapped up in the Gospel. Do not make it a side note, preach it loud and clear. I think you get the point. Let's move on to the manuscript version of this outline.

Manuscript Version of the Explanation section of the Sub-Point

Subpoint 1	We have access to God's literal words. *16 All Scripture is breathed out by God . .*

Explanation

The Bible uses phrases and words that are not natural to us. They would be understood by the original audience, but they seem a little funky now. If I said to my wife, "I'm breathing out the grocery list," she might call a doctor. Context clues would suggest that by "breathing out," I meant to speak the grocery list to her, aloud. In part of the verse, Paul is saying that all Scripture (the sixty-six books of the Bible) are the very words spoken out by God. "Breathed out" means expulsion of air by the lungs. This is God's spoken Word! (Hold up the Bible) This right here is God's actual Words! The Holy Spirit spoke out the words to the authors who wrote it down!

If this is true, it changes everything. And let me stop and say, IT IS TRUE! Since that is reality, it comes with certain implications. First, we can read the actual words of the Creator of the universe. If the president wrote you a letter, you would read it, no matter who you voted for. Well, you have the words of God right here. And since the Bible is His words, it carries authority. We do not read God's Word to ignore it, that would be foolishness! Especially because it reveals the salvation of God.

Subpoints Explanation

Subpoint 2	God's Word guides us to be different. *and profitable for teaching, for reproof, for correction, and for training in righteousness . . .*

Explanation

God does not waste His words. Every word in the Bible has power and meaning. It is there intentionally. Paul calls it "profitable." It is not a waste. Some of you had a lemonade stand growing up. Your parents paid twenty dollars to get you the supplies. Helped you set up. And you made a whole five dollars in return. That is not profitable. That is a waste. (Yes, I know the experience might be worth it, stick with me.) The Bible is not a waste.

So, if the Bible is not a waste, what is it good for? Well, Paul starts by saying it is good for teaching. This is sound doctrine. Bad doctrine and false teaching were a major issue in the church. Almost every New Testament book speaks to false teaching. It was an issue then, and it is an issue now. Look at the Prosperity Gospel preached by many modern teachers, a Gospel that says if you give money to the church or a person, God will bless you with health, wealth, and prosperity. In reality, it is sending people to Hell by the thousands. The Bible does not stop at teaching; it reproofs us. Reproofing is the exposing of error. Telling us when we are wrong. We all love that, right? Well, we should start loving it. Proverbs 12:1 states: *"Whoever loves discipline loves knowledge, but he who hates reproof is stupid."* That's pretty clear. But what do you do when you're told you're wrong? You change! The Bible is good for correction. Experiencing reproof without correction is a waste of time. That means we have to want to change. Lastly, the Bible is good for training in righteousness. This is the process of sanctification. This is the goal of the Christian. To want to be more like Christ. The Bible trains us to be more like Christ.

The truth is, the Bible does not leave anyone the same. Hebrews 4:12 says, *"For the word of God is living and active, sharper than any two-edged sword, piercing to the division of soul and of spirit, of joints and of marrow, and discerning the thoughts and intentions of the heart."* God's Word guides us to be different. But we have to want to be different.

Subpoint 3	God's Word leads us to live as God intended. *17 that the man of God may be complete, equipped for every good work.*

Explanation

If we read verse 16 without 17, it would be all about us. The Christian walk is not all about us. It is about God's impact on the world and how he uses us to make that impact. It's our living how God intended us to live from the start before we screwed it up with sin. Our sin, the sin from Adam and Eve, broke the world. It brought death, physical and spiritual, to the world. We are not righteous, and we are not complete. But the Bible leads us to righteousness through the salvation of Jesus Christ. He makes us complete. The Bible reveals salvation! The Bible leads us to salvation!

Subpoints Explanation

This is the redemptive single story of Scripture. God creates the world perfect. Adam and Eve sin and bring death and brokenness. We inherit that sin, and we continue to perpetuate that brokenness through our sin. This sin causes us to be spiritually dead. It is the punishment for sin. But God sends His son as a baby, born to a virgin. The son, Jesus, lives a perfect life but is sent to a sinner's cross to die. His death was not unplanned. Instead, His death was the plan all along. He died to take our punishment for our sins. Then, He defeated sin in the resurrection. And after spending time with His followers, He ascended to Heaven, promising to come back. The Bible tells us the truth, spoken to us by God himself. If you are not a follower of Jesus, today is the day. Romans 10:9,10 says, *"Because, if you confess with your mouth that Jesus is Lord and believe in your heart that God raised him from the dead, you will be saved. For with the heart, one believes and is justified, and with the mouth, one confesses and is saved."* In a second, I will give you the opportunity to call out to Jesus for salvation; don't waste this time.

When we are saved, we are complete. That completion is shown through our good works. The Bible equips us for those good works. It is our instruction manual on how to serve the world. This is how we live as God intended. We help heal the brokenness of the world. We live on a mission to bring the Gospel to the world!

Whew, that was some work!

Yep, that is one of the longer parts of the sermon writing process. The outline is there to guide you and keep you on track.

The application section of the subpoints goes a lot more quickly. As you can read, my manuscript follows closely to the outline, but it can and will change a little. That is why I do not typically write everything out in manuscript form. The outline helps me more than a manuscript when I'm in front of people.

 Timing: 50 Minutes

CHAPTER 16

Subpoints Application

In my sermon writing process, I have two areas for application. I give applications within the subpoints, which we are going to do here. Then, you give two to three practical overarching applications at the end of the sermon. Those are called Next Steps. They are the next steps you are asking the congregation to take. We will look at that in the next section.

The goal of this section is quickly to give a few application points that align with the specific subpoints. Remember your people here. You have men, women, children, singles, married, Christians, non-Christians, older, younger, people of different races, and people of different socio-economic statuses. While not every text you have will apply specifically to every type of person, you need to keep them all in mind. Mark Dever, author and pastor of Capitol Hill Baptist Church in Washington D.C., has an application grid[1] that I've found very helpful. I am going

---

[1] https://www.9marks.org/answer/whats-sermon-application-grid-9marks-keeps-talking-about/

to do the same thing as I did in the last section. First, I will start with the outline and then add a manuscript section. This will go surprisingly fast for many texts.

Subpoint 1	We have access to God's literal words. *16 All Scripture is breathed out by God . .*

Explanation
What does "all Scripture" mean?
This is the entire Bible (affirmed in 2 Peter 1:20-21, amongst other places.)
What does "breathed out by God" mean?
- The words "breathed out" literally mean the expulsion of air in the lungs. Or, as I like to say, spoken.
- The Bible is spoken out by God.
    The Holy Spirit speaks to the human writers, and they write it down for the people.

If this is true, what are the implications?
- In the Bible, we can read the actual words of the Creator of the universe.
- The Bible has the authority of God!
- The Bible reveals God's Salvation.
- We cannot ignore it.

Application
Simple application: you have to read the Bible daily. Make a plan. Let it change your life.

Subpoints Application

Subpoint 2	God's Word guides us to be different. *and profitable for teaching, for reproof, for correction, and for training in righteousness...*

Explanation

Define Profitable: use a mini-illustration of an unprofitable venture.

Starting a lemonade stand doesn't make money.

What is the Bible profitable for?

Teaching: This is doctrine

- Define Doctrine: Doctrine is teachings of the Christian faith. It is what we believe.
- You will get doctrine either here or somewhere else.
- This is a major issue in the early churches.
    Sixteen of the twenty-seven books of the New Testament mention false teachers.
- This is a major issue now.
    The Bible is clear that people in the church will follow doctrines that are false.
    Reference: 2 Timothy 4:3-4
    Example: Prosperity Gospel

Reproof

Reproof is exposing error.

The Bible is all about reproof.

__Proverbs 12:1:__ Whoever loves discipline loves knowledge, but he who hates reproof is stupid.

Correction

Experiencing reproof without correction is a waste of time.

- We should want change.

Training in righteousness.

This is the goal of the Christian.

- We call this sanctification.

Hebrews 4:12

> *For the word of God is living and active, sharper than any two-edged sword, piercing to the division of soul and of spirit, of joints and of marrow, and discerning the thoughts and intentions of the heart.*

The Bible guides us to be different.

Transition: We have to want to be different.

Application

Create a reading journal with action steps.
Ask three questions.

- What is God teaching me?
- Where is God reproofing me?
- How should I correct the reproof?

Subpoint 3	God's Word leads us to live as God intended. *17 that the man of God may be complete, equipped for every good work.*

Subpoints Application

Explanation

Explain the brokenness of the world.
- We are not righteous.
- We are incomplete.

The Bible leads us to salvation.
- The story of redemption
- The Gospel

    Present the Gospel of the redemptive story of the Scripture:
    - The fall
    - The Savior
    - The death
    - The resurrection and ascension
    - The return

    Romans 10:9,10

    Because, if you confess with your mouth that Jesus is Lord and believe in your heart that God raised him from the dead, you will be saved. For with the heart one believes and is justified, and with the mouth one confesses and is saved.

When we are saved, we are complete, but our completion is shown through our actions.

The Bible prepares us to be equipped for every good work.
- We live like God intended.
- We help heal the brokenness of the world.
- We bring the Gospel to the world.

Application

Are you a follower of Jesus? No, today is the day.
Are you living like a follower of Jesus? Or do you look more like the world?

Manuscript Version of the Applicataion section of the Sub-Point

Preface to the manuscript: there is an art to applications. Some applications will have specific "do this" instructions. Others will be more "believe this." Some will even be more "feel this" applications. All fit within this form as long as they fit the Scripture that we are studying. If your application for 2 Timothy 3:16,17 is tithe more, you might have missed the point. Also, I typically use the last line in the application to transition to the next point. It helps the sermon to flow. Alright, let's write the Applications manuscript.

Subpoint 1	We have access to God's literal words. *16 All Scripture is breathed out by God...*

Application

You have the voice of God written down on pages. Are you using it? If you fail to plan, you plan to fail. So, make a plan to read daily. Set a time and place and get the discipline to follow through. I promise you will not be the same if you do.

Subpoints Application

Subpoint 2	God's Word guides us to be different. *and profitable for teaching, for reproof, for correction, and for training in righteousness...*

Application

You have a plan to read. Now, what should you do while reading? Well, I forget things easily and often. The only way I remember is to write the stuff down I need to remember. So let's do that. Create a journal this week with what you've learned and your next action steps. Use 2 Timothy 3:16,17 as your guide. Ask yourself three questions every day: What is God teaching me? Where is God reproofing me? How do I correct the reproof? As we live in obedience to His Word, we start living as God intended us.

Subpoint 3	God's Word leads us to live as God intended. *17 that the man of God may be complete, equipped for every good work.*

Application

The Bible is the beautiful story of God redeeming His people. So, are you one of His people? Are you saved? Are you a follower of Jesus? If the answer is no, today is the day. At the end of the sermon, you will have an opportunity to respond to the call of Jesus.

If you are a follower, if someone looked at your life, would they know? Do you look more like the world or like Jesus? If I asked your five closest friends what was most important in your life, what would they say? How we live and what we do shows the world that we follow Jesus. If our lives are saturated with God's Word, we will serve others. We are doing the good works that we are equipped to do. That means our primary responsibility will be sharing the Gospel with a broken world.

Not too bad!

That section is always a lot of fun. It should convict you as well as your church. It is like you are pouring out what God has been teaching you all week. In the next section, the last task of Tuesday, you will finish out with two to three Next Steps. Then you will rest. It has been a long day so far.

 Timing: 20 Minutes

CHAPTER 17

Next Steps

When I was seven, I was watching *Star Trek: Next Generation* with my dad. Geordi La Forge, played by LeVar Burton, made a model of an old wooden ship for a visiting captain that he served under. I was amazed. He built that ship. I became obsessed with models. I desperately wanted to build a model car. At a swap meet about a month later, my dad and I saw a box for a model car on sale. It was a Dodge Viper, the coolest car I'd ever scene. He bought it for me. I couldn't wait to put it together. So, when I got home, I ripped opened the box with urgency, only to find a bunch of blue plastic pieces. I'd never built a model. I didn't know that you only get plastic pieces that have to be glued together. I didn't know that you then had to buy paint and paint it yourself. I thought it was going to be easy. I stared at it with no idea what the next step was.

    We can preach a great sermon. We can yell. We can cry. We can make them cry. But if they don't know what to do with the sermon after they leave, we've just wasted their time. The Next Steps section of the sermon is simple: give them a couple of things to do when they get home. I typically use questions four and five from the Preaching Preparation Document to guide those next steps. Here are our answers:

1. **What do you want them to feel?**
   An appreciation for God's Word and a desire to read and follow it.
2. **What do you want them to do?**
   Create a daily reading plan.

Let's use those to craft our next steps:

Next Steps

1. **Daily, thank God for giving us His Word.**
2. **Create a daily reading and journaling plan.**
3. **If you don't know Jesus, today is the day.**

Finished!

Alright, you've finished your Day two! Now go do other pastor stuff.

 **Timing:** 10 Minutes

Total timing for the day:
1 hours 55 minutes

Next Steps

Sermon Outline So Far

Here is an updated outline for the day. The updated manuscript will be in the last chapter, Chapter twenty-three.

Series:	Faithful Church
Text:	2 Timothy 3:16,17
Sermon Date:	1/01/2075
Big Idea:	God's Word transforms us.
Intro	
Reading	*2 Timothy 3:16,17* **16** *All Scripture is breathed out by God and profitable for teaching, for reproof, for correction, and for training in righteousness,* **17** *that the man of God may be complete, equipped for every good work.* **Pastor:** This is the Word of the Lord **All:** Thanks be to God
The case for the Big Idea	

There is one constant in this world. It is change. We are not created to be stagnant. Our bodies change. Our personalities change. Our beliefs change. Even as followers of Jesus, our theology changes and matures. However, there is definitely change that is not good. And you have a choice of what will ultimately transform you.

This question was one of the largest issues in the early church. A man named Paul went throughout the Middle East, Europe, and parts of Asia, preached the Gospel, and started churches. One of his favorite churches is in a city named Ephesus. Ephesus was a major trade and religious center in Rome. Ephesus had a large temple dedicated to Artemis, the Roman Goddess. It was one of the seven wonders of the ancient world. People would come from all over to worship there. And yet God used Paul to plant this church.

Paul loved this church, he sent his favorite pupil, Timothy, to pastor this church. He writes this church one of the most theologically significant letters, *Letter to the Ephesians*. Paul sets this church up to succeed the best he can, but the world does not stop its pursuit to transform us.

The church quickly came under attack by false doctrines. The Jews wanted the church to return to legalism. The Gnostics were speaking out against the divinity of Jesus. The Roman pagans were trying to push these new believers back to idol worship. The church was under attack. So, Paul writes Timothy. He actually writes him twice. In the first letter he organizes the church. In this second letter, Paul's last letter, he is telling Pastor Timothy to protect the church from false doctrine. He doesn't want the church to be transformed by the world. He wants the world to be transformed by Christ's church.

How does Paul protect the church? He grounds its people in the only Word of the God that we have. He tells them that the only godly transformation happens through the Holy Spirit speaking to them through the Word of God.

The truth is that the world is still trying to transform us. If you're a Christian, the world is constantly pulling you to your old nature. We still have false idols, false doctrines, and worldly passions that try to change us. But it is our choice of what we will allow to transform us. Will we go back to our old selves and live in the prison that Christ has freed us from? Or will we be transformed by His Holy Word?

God has spoken, why waste it? The Bible is not just a book that gives us good morals; it has the ability to transform us! So, what do you want to influence your life? Because *God's Word transforms us.* Today, we will be answering the following questions: *How does God's Word transform us?*

Question for the Big Idea	How does God's Word transform us?
Subpoint 1	We have access to God's literal words. *16 All Scripture is breathed out by God . .*
Explanation	

What does "all Scripture" mean?

This is the entire Bible (affirmed in 2 Peter 1:20-21, amongst other places.)

What does "breathed out by God" mean?

- The words "breathed out" literally mean the expulsion of air in the lungs. Or, as I like to say, spoken.
- The Bible is spoken out by God.
    The Holy Spirit speaks to the human writers, and they write it down for the people.

If this is true, what are the implications?
- In the Bible, we can read the actual words of the Creator of the universe.
- The Bible has the authority of God!
- The Bible reveals God's Salvation.
- We cannot ignore it.

Illustration	
Application	

Simple application: you have to read the Bible daily. Make a plan. Let it change your life.

Subpoint 2	God's Word guides us to be different. *and profitable for teaching, for reproof, for correction, and for training in righteousness...*
Explanation	

Define Profitable: use a mini-illustration of an unprofitable venture.

Starting a lemonade stand doesn't make money.

What is the Bible profitable for?

Teaching: This is doctrine
- Define Doctrine: Doctrine is teachings of the Christian faith. It is what we believe.
- You will get doctrine either here or somewhere else.
- This is a major issue in the early churches.
    Sixteen of the twenty-seven books of the New Testament mention false teachers.

- This is a major issue now.

    The Bible is clear that people in the church will follow doctrines that are false.

    Reference: 2 Timothy 4:3-4

    Example: Prosperity Gospel

Reproof

Reproof is exposing error.

The Bible is all about reproof.

> ***Proverbs 12:1:*** *Whoever loves discipline loves knowledge, but he who hates reproof is stupid.*

Correction

Experiencing reproof without correction is a waste of time.

- We should want change.

Training in righteousness.

This is the goal of the Christian.

- We call this sanctification.

Hebrews 4:12

> *For the word of God is living and active, sharper than any two-edged sword, piercing to the division of soul and of spirit, of joints and of marrow, and discerning the thoughts and intentions of the heart.*

The Bible guides us to be different.

Transition: We have to want to be different.

Illustration	

Application

Create a reading journal with action steps.
Ask three questions.
- What is God teaching me?
- Where is God reproofing me?
- How should I correct the reproof?

Subpoint 3	God's Word leads us to live as God intended. *17 that the man of God may be complete, equipped for every good work.*

Explanation

Explain the brokenness of the world.
- We are not righteous.
- We are incomplete.

The Bible leads us to salvation.
- The story of redemption
- The Gospel
    Present the Gospel of the redemptive story of the Scripture:
    - The fall
    - The Savior
    - The death
    - The resurrection and ascension
    - The return

Next Steps

Romans 10:9,10
> *Because, if you confess with your mouth that Jesus is Lord and believe in your heart that God raised him from the dead, you will be saved. For with the heart one believes and is justified, and with the mouth one confesses and is saved.*

When we are saved, we are complete, but our completion is shown through our actions.

The Bible prepares us to be equipped for every good work.
- We live like God intended.
- We help heal the brokenness of the world.
- We bring the Gospel to the world.

Illustration	
Application	

Are you a follower of Jesus? No, today is the day.
Are you living like a follower of Jesus? Or do you look more like the world?

Next Steps	

1. Daily, thank God for giving us His Word.
2. Create a daily reading and journaling plan.
3. If you don't know Jesus, today is the day.

Outro	
Prayer	

WEDNESDAY
Day Three

CHAPTER 18

Why Spend a Day on Coloring?

I recently pastored a church in Napa, California. There were vineyards that opened up to mountains behind the small townhouse that we owned. It was an unbelievable site. We would often take drives up Highway 29 in awe of the beauty of God's creation. There's a river near the region that comes from a large lake. Once a week, a few of my church elders and I would put our waders on and go fly-fishing, enjoying the coolness of the water, the heat of the sun, and the fresh air. We do not live in a utilitarian world. We live in a world filled with color. A world that looks like an illustration. If this is our world, why is our preaching so different? Why do we subject our people to preaching that is colorless and dull? We have to do better.

That is why we spend an entire day coloring our sermons. By coloring, I mean adding an Intro in the beginning, an Outro at the end, and illustrations throughout. We think about the heart of our people. We look to connect the text to their personal lives, lives lived in color. The writers of the Bible, the Holy Spirit, and the human authors, understood the need for color in the text. There are obvious examples in the Psalms and parables. But even the purpose of books like Genesis, recounting creation and establishing the Israelites, is filled with beauty and shocking imagery. God created using color, so let us color our sermons.

To those guys, you know who you are, who think illustrations are scary, I know. Illustrations *are* scary. I know they feel like a waste of time. A good expositor doesn't need to wade in the waters of illustrations. That line is purposefully an illustration! Can I give you some advice? I'll give it in terms of a *Mad* TV skit from 2001. Bob Newhart is working as a psychologist and a new patient comes in. He tells the patient that the visit is only five dollars because it will only last five minutes. The new patient, stunned, agrees to the terms. She starts describing her problems. They are, of course, crazy and extreme. Bob Newhart listens for a few minutes, then simply says two words, and he has her write them down: "Stop it!"

Stop belittling illustrations. You need them. They make you a better preacher. And if you follow certain rules, which I will lay out, they will be faithful to the text. Alright, let's go color that sermon.

Everybody has a couch

When I first started preaching, the goal of my illustrations was to show either how interesting my life had been or how smart I really was. So, I would sit and think of the most fantastic stories of my young life. As a middle-class kid who grew up in a small town in Arizona, my life did not have many great stories. So, when

Why Spend a Day on Coloring

those stories would run out, I would study history, technology, or something of the like to show my church how educated I was. My illustrations were long and fanciful. They would be about World War II squadrons or heroes in the ancient world. My pride was in my stories, even when they weren't mine. Then the day came when I didn't have a story. I couldn't come up with the right illustration. As my disappointment grew, the time ticked down, and I had to preach. So, I relented and used my placeholder illustration.

Now, this illustration was not my intro or outro. This was a middleman, something to highlight a specific concept in the sermon. The text was Hebrews 12. The concept was the uncomfortable nature of the Holy Spirit's discipline. Our changed life is different from our previous dead nature, and when God calls us into change, it can be difficult. The illustration went something like this:

> *I love Costco. It's my favorite store. On my days off, I often just walk the aisles. It's a lesson in not giving into temptation—except when you do. I bought a couch. I bought a couch without my wife. I was walking through Costco, and I saw the couch, and before I could even second guess what I was doing, it was in my truck. Although I wanted to blame the allure of Costco, it was my fault, and I needed to admit my financial blunder to my wife. I made the call, and she was very gracious, but she did leave me with one remark: 'Well, that's your couch now.' There was no going back. I got home, set up the couch, and took my first ceremonious sit. As I sat down, I quickly came to the conclusion that this was the most*

uncomfortable couch of all time. But it's now 'my couch,' and I had to live with it. So, I made the decision to sit in the same spot every day. As I sat in the same spot, it became more and more comfortable. Soon, it became the most comfortable seat in the house. It was my favorite place to be." Here's the transition: "As we first sit in the Holy Spirit, we are going to be uncomfortable. We may even ask why we would want to follow a God that makes us uncomfortable. But in that moment, you have a choice: will you get up and stop listening or dedicate yourself to the God that saved you? I guarantee this: as you listen and move your life to Him, it will be the only place you'll ever want to be.

I preached the rest of the sermon. The intro and outro were about World War II. I spent a lot of time researching it. I got off the pulpit and did the same thing I've done since I started preaching, asked my wife how it went. Expecting an overwhelming appreciation for the history I just presented, she said only one thing, "I loved the couch illustration." I was more than mildly irritated. I couldn't believe that was what she took away. When I asked her why, she simply said: "Because everybody has a couch."

Illustrations are not just for *you*. They are to highlight the text for your people. They exist to take a difficult concept and make it easy for your people to understand through a simple story. Does that mean they cannot be fanciful? Absolutely not. But if your illustrations are above your people, they lose their efficacy. They no longer serve their purpose. So, as we get deeper into the process of writing our illustrations, remember, everybody has a couch.

Rules for Illustrations

Before we start writing the illustration, we have to go over the rules. The rules of illustrations are important. They make sure to keep us from sounding like doofuses and confusing the congregation. Here are the rules:

1. **You are not the hero.**
2. **The goal is to highlight the text, not you.**
3. **Be specific.**
4. **Be vulnerable, but not weird.**
5. **Do not lie.**
6. **Illustrations about your life are best.**

Simple Sermons

1. You are not the hero.

We all want to be the hero. No one dreams at night about being the crew member wearing a red shirt in "Star Trek;" we want to be Captain Kirk or Spock. That is great in normal life, it's terrible on stage. In fact, it's sinful at the pulpit. Pastors already have to deal with the temptation of ego. We have a platform, and people listen to us (for the most part). It's difficult to keep our pride in check. But we have to in our preaching. I was listening to a sermon from a guy preaching his first sermon at a new church he was leading. His first illustration was about how he made a shot over a future NBA player. It was lame. It added nothing to the sermon. It had no reason to be there except that it made him look like a hero. A preacher I listened to quite a few times would always tell the same story. He was in the Air Force and saved a bunch of people's lives when an airplane engine malfunctioned. Cool story, but it didn't have anything to do with the text. He used it every time he preached. It was his hero story. *You are not the hero* of your sermon, Jesus is. So don't illustrate like it. Do not be the one teaching other people lessons in your story. Do not be the one who saves lives. Do not be the hero. Instead, be on the other end. Be the person who learns the lesson. Be the person who made the mistake. Show that you are real and that God is teaching you to be more like Him. Do not be the hero.

2. The goal is to highlight the Text, not you.

The worst part of both the NBA and the airplane story is that they had nothing to do with the text. They highlighted the preacher. Let me be blunt: you are not worth highlighting compared to the Word of God. Our illustrations exist to take a difficult concept and make it more attainable to our people. That is what stories do. Instead of only talking about how difficult the Christian walk is, Paul compares it to running a race with endurance. This is an illustration. It's hard to understand the abstract idea of how difficult it is to run the Christian walk, but we all understand how terrible running is. The goal of any illustration is to highlight the text.

3. Be specific.

This one could also be "Learn to tell a good, succinct story." Many pastors and speakers do not work on their storytelling abilities, so their illustrations typically turn into an "It's like that old Andy Griffin show. You remember that?" I actually heard that once. It wasn't the start of an illustration, it *was* the illustration. A good story has specifics: names, places, surroundings, and descriptions. Knowing this will help your listeners connect to the story. Caution: too much specific information can be overwhelming and time-consuming. The duration for giving any illustration is less than two minutes. I suggest finding someone and practicing your illustrations.

4. Be vulnerable but not weird.

Why do some many pastors break the "don't be a hero" rule? Because they are afraid of vulnerability. They have to seem like the expert or the strongest person in the room. It's not good. Your people need to hear vulnerable stories. They need to hear about their pastor's struggles. They need to hear when you have failed.

Be vulnerable, but don't be weird. We've all heard the person who's gone up and told the story that we knew shouldn't have been told. The weird one. The one that gave too much information. Yeah, don't do that. When you are vulnerable, you will make people uncomfortable. There is a bad type of uncomfortable. An uncomfortable that takes away from the text. Don't be weird.

5. Do not lie.

This one seems obvious, right? People get caught doing this all the time. They tell a story that isn't theirs. They make up a story that didn't happen. This is lying, and you don't need to do it. Illustrations are not about having the greatest stories ever told. Most pastors live boring lives, but so do your people! The good storytellers make the normal applicable. You don't need to lie, so don't do it. Remember, everybody has a couch.

6. Illustrations about your life are best.

I love to talk about history, especially if I just looked it up and very few people know about it. I feel smart and empowered. But smart and empowered doesn't help my sermons. People connect best with personal and real stories. They can take those illustrations and place them in their own life, which is why we are giving an illustration. It is why everyone connected to the dumb couch story. It doesn't mean that you can't use history or something similar, but many times it will not connect so well. People don't normally have a frame of reference for those types of illustrations. I encourage pastors of new congregations to tell stories about their lives, especially in the first eight weeks. It allows the congregation to get to know you.

Why Spend a Day on Coloring

How to write an illustration

A brilliant writer, teacher, and pastor, Jared C. Wilson, once said at a conference I attended, "Every pastor should have about an hour a week where they stare out the window and dream up illustrations." Illustrations need to take time. They need to breathe. You need to understand where you are going with the illustration. You need to know how to land the illustration so it actually makes sense. Wednesday is a day of dreaming and thinking through the heart of your sermon. You are looking into your own life. The experiences you've had. How this text has been demonstrated in your own life. Illustrations are a beautiful part of the sermon writing process. But they can also be daunting. Where do they go? How do I write them? There is no exact science to this, but since I like routine so much, here is where I start. This is how I write an illustration:

Know what you want to illustrate

I typically give one illustration per subpoint. While this is not a hard and fast rule, it helps to create a baseline of need. The illustration typically comes at the beginning or right after the explanation section of the subpoint. The goal is to illustrate the purpose of the subpoint but can also transition from the subpoint to the application. Let's use the first subpoint in the 2 Timothy sermon as an example: We have access to God's literal words. The explanation goes through what "all Scripture" and "breathed out" means. Those areas seem pretty self-evident. The other section of the explanation speaks to the authority of God's Word. This can be a little difficult to understand. Let's write an illustration based on that idea.

Know the goal before you write the illustration

Isn't the goal to tell them that God's Word carries authority? Well, yes and no. The goal of our illustration needs to be more specific. What exactly is our story going to do? I think to the times that other letters or notes have carried authority. Teacher's notes or, worse yet, principal's notes. The notes carry authority from the school to the parents. I think our goal should be a story that demonstrates how the authority of someone else's writing pales in comparison to the Word of God. I think I got one.

Let's illustrate the sermon.

My first few years in college were rough. I would rather go out with friends than go to school. This mentality led to five colleges in two years with a lot of school debt. One school where I got academically relieved of my duties was Arizona State University. If you know ASU, you know that it is virtually impossible to get academically kicked out of the school. That first semester, I learned that I could do the nearly impossible. I didn't buy books, and I barely went to classes. At the end of the semester, my GPA was less than 1. Then I got a letter from the registrar signed by the dean saying something to this effect: "College might not be for you. Don't come back." That might not be a direct quote, but it was something similar. I couldn't ignore this note and just start going back to school. Why? Because the dean and the registrar had the authority to remove me from ASU. These were words that carried weight. What they said was implemented. I read it with finality.

We can easily understand the authority of a school official, but why are we so flippant about the Word of God? We read it like a hobby. We write notes and make commitments we never intend to follow through on. We live as if these words do not have authority, yet they are the ultimate authority.

Review of the illustration

Yes, it's a true story. This really happened. The illustration is quick and gets to the point. We understand that other's words have authority, but we don't recognize the authority of God's Word. Notice that it shows vulnerability yet is light-hearted. I am not the hero; I am the one learning the lesson. It's a simple illustration that highlights the point of the text. Now, we just need to do it three more times.

 Timing for all illustrations : 1 Hour

CHAPTER 19

Intro and Outro

The day I learned the importance of an intro and outro I was not able to attend the MLK50 event held by the Gospel Coalition. But I did sit in my office in Napa and watch most of it. One of my favorite sermons was preached that day. Dr. Russell Moore got to the podium, looking like the most Southern Baptist guy in the world, and after a brief introduction and reading of the Word, said, "There's a wreath at the Lorraine Motel." A weird and somewhat unimpressive way to start a sermon. Dr. Moore then preaches for thirty-five minutes. It's a beautiful sermon. Then, he gets to the end, and the crescendo begins. And then he ends, "The Gospel is alive, God is at work, but for now, there are wreathes at the Lorraine Motel." I would encourage you to listen to this sermon. I can barely type the words without tearing up. It was that day that I realized the power of the introduction and outro.

Don't waste your first and last words.

Growing up, I had a pastor who always started the same way. He would get up to the pulpit, take a drink of water, and then tell us a joke. The joke was always stupid. The people would always give a pity laugh, to which he would say something like "Come on, that was funny." Then the man would pivot to the Word of God. He would preach for forty-five minutes and then, at some point, would stop and say, "That's all the time I have; let's pray." How many sermons do I remember of his? None. While his intro and outro were not the main culprits, they stand out. He didn't take the beginning and ending seriously; why would we take anything else he said seriously? The intro and outro are more than getting the sermon car started; they are the book ends of the sermon. They set up the expectation of what's to come and send you home with what's important. Don't waste your first and last words.

Preaching is an art that we should constantly strive to improve.

I love comedians. I believe they are the pinnacle of public speaking. They walk into a room of people who expect them to make them laugh. The pressure is incredible. What I love even more about comedians is the practice and hard work they put into their craft. The good ones write the material, perform the material, and then change the material. The really good ones can take an hour and start a joke in the first minutes that doesn't pay off until the last joke. It's beautiful. It's something that I watch for in comedians. Why do they take the time and effort to make their act better? Because it is their craft. It is their art. Why are we different? Why do we get to settle? We don't.

Intro and Outro

We are called to do the same. We are called to give everything we have when we write, prepare, and deliver the sermon. This care and work hit throughout the sermon but are shown most in our intro and outro.

Definition of Intro and Outro

The intro and outro are simple: the beginning and end of the sermon. I purposely chose to write about them in one chapter because I believe they are linked together. While they are illustrations, they are not only illustrations: they are more. The intro and outro are what most people will remember of the sermon, so we must treat them that way. We must put time, effort, and care into our intro and outro.

Let's write our intro and outro

Like everything else, the Intro and Outro start with our Big Idea of the sermon and the text: God's Word transforms us. That's what we need to introduce, and that's how we need to land the plane. If we look at the intro and outro as two sides of one coin, then we need to write them together. They will play off each other. They should relate to the same story. Transformation is the major action happening in this text. Let's use that word to develop our intro and outro. I don't want to tell a story of my own transformation because of the Word - that is a little too overly direct. What else transforms? As I write this, I'm looking outside of my home office at an abandoned garage; yes, it drives me crazy. Buildings often go through major transformations. We all have stories of old buildings that change. In fact, you could argue that buildings cannot stay stagnant, they either improve or decay. (Yes, I'm writing this in real time) Let's go with it.

The Intro for 2 Timothy

Since I was young, I've loved old broken-down buildings. I grew up in a small town in Arizona on the Colorado River, Lake Havasu City. The city had a boom in the 1970s and then another boom in the 1990s/2000s. That meant there were a lot of buildings from the 1970s that laid dormant. There was one old apartment building. I loved driving by that old building. It had this incredible sign that still halfway lit up at night. It was old. It was gross. As much as I loved the sign, the building needed some type of intervention. After I moved away for college, I came home one summer, and I was amazed. This building that had broken down for so many decades was completely new. Someone came in and bought the land and rebuilt the apartments from the ground up. They were transformed, it was incredible.

God is not an improvement for our lives, he completely changes us from the ground up. He makes us new. And through His Word, He continues to transform us. We are not stagnant, and we are not in decay. Instead, we are being transformed. *God's Word transforms us.*

The Outro for 2 Timothy

When I go visit my hometown, I often drive by that building. The new owners repaired and left that old sign. I often think about what that old building would look like now if it had not been transformed. See, buildings do not lie stagnant. They are either in a constant state of rebuilding or in decay. The elements of the world do not allow stagnation. And that is true for our own life. You may think that you can maintain, but you can't. You are either in a state of decay or transforming to be like Christ. While the Holy Spirit is executing this transformation, His primary means of that transformation is the Bible. That means you are either reading, studying, and applying Scripture or watching your spiritual walk erode. Don't waste this time. If you are not a follower of Jesus, repent and believe. Allow God to transform you into a new creation. Allow God to further your transformation through His Word. If you are a follower of Jesus, live in His Word and see the fruit that God produces through our transformation.

Review

This sermon's intro and outro are simple, but they convey the message. They strike the listener and bring the sermon to action points. They are not necessarily emotional, although some intros and outros will be. They get the message across. They bookend what we want them to hear. The intro brings in the idea of the broken-down apartment building getting transformed. The outro finishes the idea that stagnation is not an option. You either transform or decay. Alright, the sermon is done.

 **Timing:** 30 Minutes

Total timing for the day:
1 hours 30 minutes
Total timing for sermon:
5 hours 50 minutes

CHAPTER 20

Rest and Preach

Our sermon is written. Now, what do you do for the rest of the week? You rest. You work. You pay attention to your church members. You tell someone about Jesus. You take a nap. Go get a workout in. You check in with your staff. Talk to your kids. Go on a date with your wife. Just don't go back and work on that sermon. Trust the process. Trust your work. You'll check it one more time on Sunday. But for now, go do the other things you need to do as a pastor.

Time audit

My role at our church is to pastor the pastors. In that role, I often find the same mistakes are being made time and time again. They are the same mistakes that I've made throughout my ministry career. One of our campus pastors was struggling. The campus was in decline. Something wasn't right. At our church, all of our campus pastors are expected to preach every week. So, I

Simple Sermons

asked my campus pastor to give me a time audit. He was to write down what he did every day of the week. The time audit revealed that he spent over fifty percent of the time working on his sermon. He only met with one group of church members a week, a midweek Bible study that he led. His job was his sermon. He didn't smell like the sheep he was shepherding. That needed to change.

Pastor and leader, in order to smell like your sheep, you need to be with them. You need to visit them. You need to sit with visitors. You need to be in the community, inviting people to church. You need to be sharing the Gospel. Pastoring a church is not rocket science. It is about you and the people. Your sermon is not worth much if you have no one to preach it to. So, what do you do with the rest of your week? *You pastor.* Go get it done.

CHAPTER 21

What Do I Do On Sunday?

I wake up. I do my normal routine. I eat the same breakfast. I drink the same amount of coffee. Then I go to the church. I meet with the band and pray with them. Then, while the band is practicing, I go to my office and look at my sermon for the first time in days. I did not look at it on Friday or Saturday. Those are the days I dedicate to rest and the family. So, I look at the sermon. I'll typically put it in a PDF and then write on it using an iPad and Apple Pencil. That's not a promotion for them, if they would like to sponsor me, awesome. But if you prefer, you can print it out and write on it directly. I might make a few adjustments. I might change a few words. But for the most part, the sermon is left unchanged. I practice the intro and outro. I work through the case for the Big Idea. I pray through my daily liturgy. Then, I trust that I've done the work and that the Holy Spirit has guided me through the process. I get to the lobby fifteen minutes early. I shake as many hands as possible. I check in with the sheep. I worship in the front row. Then I get up there and preach. I give it my all. The work is done. I go home, eat lunch, and take a nap. I do any other things that the church needs on Sunday. I go to bed and get ready to start the process over again. I love it.

You don't have to follow my Sundays. Catch your own rhythm. But let me give a few semi-rigid rules:

1. **Don't rewrite your sermon on Thursday, Friday, Saturday, or Sunday.** I've only done that twice in twenty years because of extreme circumstances. The sermon is done, trust the process.
2. **Repent. Confess your sins.** Call and make up with your wife for the fight you got into last night. Get your heart right.
3. **Be with your people.** If your church is less than 200 people, you should shake every single hand in the church. If it is more, then make sure you shake as many as you can. If the time-killer comes to tell you everything about his life, ask to plan a day the next week to have coffee with him. Since you now practice this sermon writing process, you'll have plenty of time.
4. **Preach with everything you have.** Don't leave anything on the table. Give it your all.

The Gift of Preaching

Preaching is an art, a process, a discipline, an honor, and a gift. God has called you to do something incredible: expose His Word to His People. This gift is tremendous and should never be taken for granted. We have the greatest job in the world.

CHAPTER 22

You Did It!
Now Let's Get Ready for Next Week

I left a very healthy church with several pastors who shared the preaching responsibilities in Phoenix to take on a church revitalization in Napa, California. In Phoenix, I preached about thirty-six to forty weeks a year. During my first year in Napa, I preached fifty-one weeks. This is too much, but it was the reality of my situation. As soon as I was through preaching, I was already thinking about next week's sermon. Why? Because *Sunday is always coming.*

The median church size is less than seventy people.[2] That means that the majority of pastors reading this book pastor a church of less than one hundred people. With a church of less than one hundred people, you are preaching a lot. Why? Because it is doubtful that you have or can afford a second preacher. There are two reasons this book is for you.

---

[2] https://churchrenew.org/emerging-trends-in-congregations/

Reason One

This book is here to help you find a healthy rhythm in preaching. You have a lot of responsibilities, and preaching preparation needs to be both a joy as well as an additional burden. A three-day preparation timeline will help you keep that joy intact throughout the marathon of ministry.

Reason Two

You need to train up more preachers in your church, and this book will assist them. Preaching does not require a secret skill set only taught in a seminary. Preaching is about diligence, heart, call, and methods. This book provides a straightforward method to train up new preachers. I've employed this method countless times to help young preachers. Train up some new leaders and get some rest!

Sunday is Coming

Those words either comfort or bring anxiety. But it is the reality. If God has called you, you can do it. You've done it already. Take this method, make it a routine, and watch what God will do with your preaching.

CHAPTER 23

The Stuff at the End

A quick word before we look at the sermon. I wrote this sermon as I wrote this book. It was done in real time. Although I have preached this text before, I didn't use any prior notes. So, this sermon is fresh. Also, as we look at the finished sermon, you'll notice I've added two other illustrations for the two other subpoints. In the outline, I just gave the words that I would use to help me recall the illustration. In the manuscript, I wrote out the illustration. The sermon was completed on Wednesday, day three. So, let's take a look at both the complete outline and the sermon manuscript.

Finished Sermon Outline

Series:	Faithful Church
Text:	2 Timothy 3:16,17
Sermon Date:	1/01/2075
Big Idea:	God's Word transforms us.
Intro	The old apartments in Lake Havasu and the transformation that happened.
Reading	*2 Timothy 3:16,17* **16** *All Scripture is breathed out by God and profitable for teaching, for reproof, for correction, and for training in righteousness,* **17** *that the man of God may be complete, equipped for every good work.* **Pastor:** This is the Word of the Lord **All:** Thanks be to God

The case for the Big Idea

- Change is the constant in the world. What is going to change you?
- The early church, Paul, and planting the church at Ephesus.
- Timothy (pastor at Ephesus) and the struggles in the early church.
- Paul fights false doctrines with the Word of God.
- We are still dealing with the same issues.
- God has spoken, why waste it?

The Stuff at the End

- So, what do you want to influence your life? Because *God's Word transforms us.* And today we will be answering: *How does God's Word transform us?*

Question for the Big Idea	How does God's Word transform us?
Subpoint 1	We have access to God's literal words. *16 All Scripture is breathed out by God . .*
Explanation	

What does "all Scripture" mean?

This is the entire Bible (affirmed in 2 Peter 1:20-21, amongst other places.)

What does "breathed out by God" mean?

- The words "breathed out" literally mean the expulsion of air in the lungs. Or, as I like to say, spoken.
- The Bible is spoken out by God.
    The Holy Spirit speaks to the human writers, and they write it down for the people.

If this is true, what are the implications?

- In the Bible, we can read the actual words of the Creator of the universe.
- The Bible has the authority of God!
- The Bible reveals God's Salvation.
- We cannot ignore it.

Illustration	College and the authority of the dean's note.

Application

Simple application: you have to read the Bible daily. Make a plan. Let it change your life.

Subpoint 2	God's Word guides us to be different. *and profitable for teaching, for reproof, for correction, and for training in righteousness...*

Explanation

Define Profitable: use a mini-illustration of an unprofitable venture.

Starting a lemonade stand doesn't make money.

What is the Bible profitable for?

Teaching: This is doctrine

- Define Doctrine: Doctrine is teachings of the Christian faith. It is what we believe.
- You will get doctrine either here or somewhere else.
- This is a major issue in the early churches.
    Sixteen of the twenty-seven books of the New Testament mention false teachers.
- This is a major issue now.
    The Bible is clear that people in the church will follow doctrines that are false.
    Reference: 2 Timothy 4:3-4
    Example: Prosperity Gospel

Reproof

Reproof is exposing error.

The Bible is all about reproof.

The Stuff at the End

> ***Proverbs 12:1:*** *Whoever loves discipline loves knowledge, but he who hates reproof is stupid.*

Correction

Experiencing reproof without correction is a waste of time.

- We should want change.

Training in righteousness.

This is the goal of the Christian.

- We call this sanctification.

Hebrews 4:12

> *For the word of God is living and active, sharper than any two-edged sword, piercing to the division of soul and of spirit, of joints and of marrow, and discerning the thoughts and intentions of the heart.*

The Bible guides us to be different.

Transition: We have to want to be different.

Illustration	Forty years old, and the decision to work out.
Application	

Create a reading journal with action steps.

Ask three questions.

- What is God teaching me?
- Where is God reproofing me?
- How should I correct the reproof?

Subpoint 3	God's Word leads us to live as God intended. *17 that the man of God may be complete, equipped for every good work.*

Explanation

Explain the brokenness of the world.
- We are not righteous.
- We are incomplete.

The Bible leads us to salvation.

- The story of redemption
- The Gospel

    Present the Gospel of the redemptive story of the Scripture:
    - The fall
    - The Savior
    - The death
    - The resurrection and ascension
    - The return

    Romans 10:9,10

    Because, if you confess with your mouth that Jesus is Lord and believe in your heart that God raised him from the dead, you will be saved. For with the heart one believes and is justified, and with the mouth one confesses and is saved.

When we are saved, we are complete, but our completion is shown through our actions.

The Stuff at the End

The Bible prepares us to be equipped for every good work.
- We live like God intended.
- We help heal the brokenness of the world.
- We bring the Gospel to the world.

Illustration	Continuation of gym illustration. I didn't know what to do. How to lift? I could barely run.

Application

Are you a follower of Jesus? No, today is the day.
Are you living like a follower of Jesus? Or do you look more like the world?

Next Steps

1. Daily, thank God for giving us His Word.
2. Create a daily reading and journaling plan.
3. If you don't know Jesus, today is the day.

Outro	Back to the old apartment building in Hvasu. We cannot stay stagnant; we will either transform or decay. The word of God transforms us through the power of the Holy Spirit.
Prayer	• For people to follow Jesus • For us to submit to God's Word.

Finished Sermon Manuscript

Series:	Faithful Church
Text:	2 Timothy 3:16,17
Sermon Date:	1/01/2075
Big Idea:	God's Word transforms us.

Intro

Since I was young, I've loved old broken-down buildings. I grew up in a small town in Arizona on the Colorado River, Lake Havasu City. The city had a boom in the 1970s and then another boom in the 1990s and 2000s. That meant there were a lot of buildings from the 1970s that lay dormant. There was one old apartment building. I loved driving by that old building. It had this incredible sign that would still halfway light up at night. It was old. It was gross. As much as I loved the sign, the building needed some type of intervention. After I moved away for college, I came home one summer, and I was amazed. This building that had broken down for so many decades was completely new. Someone came in and bought the land and rebuilt the apartments from the ground up. They were transformed, it was incredible.

God is not an improvement for our lives, He completely changes us from the ground up. He makes us new. And through His Word, He continues to transform us. We are not stagnant and we are not in decay. Instead, we are being transformed. *God's Word transforms us.*

The Stuff at the End

Reading	**2 Timothy 3:16,17**
	16 *All Scripture is breathed out by God and profitable for teaching, for reproof, for correction, and for training in righteousness,* **17** *that the man of God may be complete, equipped for every good work.*
	Pastor: This is the Word of the Lord
	All: Thanks be to God

The Case for the Big Idea

There is one constant in this world, it is change. We are not created to be stagnant. Our bodies change. Our personalities change. Our beliefs change. Even as followers of Jesus, our theology changes and matures. However, there is definitely change that is not good. And you have a choice of what will ultimately transform you.

This question was one of the largest issues in the early church. A man named Paul went throughout the Middle East, Europe, and parts of Asia, preached the Gospel, and started churches. One of his favorite churches was in a city named Ephesus. Ephesus was a major trade and religious center in Rome. Ephesus had a large temple dedicated to Artemis, the Roman Goddess. It was one of the seven wonders of the ancient world. People would come from all over to worship there. And yet God used Paul to plant this church.

Paul loved this church, he sent his favorite pupil, Timothy, to pastor this church. He writes this church one of the most theologically significant letters, *Letter to the Ephesians*. Paul sets this church up to succeed the best he can, but the world does not stop its pursuit to transform us.

The church quickly came under attack by false doctrines. The Jews wanted the church to return to legalism. The Gnostics were speaking out against the divinity of Jesus. The Roman pagans were trying to push these new believers back to idol worship. The church was under attack. So, Paul writes Timothy. He actually writes him twice. In the first letter he organizes the church. In this second letter, Paul's last letter, he is telling Pastor Timothy to protect the church from false doctrine. He doesn't want the church to be transformed by the world. He wants the world to be transformed by Christ's church.

How does Paul protect the church? He grounds its people in the only Word of the God that we have. He tells them that the only godly transformation happens through the Holy Spirit speaking to them through the Word of God.

The truth is that the world is still trying to transform us. If you're a Christian, the world is constantly pulling you to your old nature. We still have false idols, false doctrines, and worldly passions that try to change us. But it is our choice of what we will allow to transform us. Will we go back to our old selves and live in the prison that Christ has freed us from? Or will he be transformed by His Holy Word?

God has spoken, why waste it? The Bible is not just a book that gives us good morals; it has the ability to transform us! So, what do you want to influence your life? Because *God's Word transforms us*. And today we will be answering: *How does God's Word transform us?*

The Stuff at the End

Question for the Big Idea	How does God's Word transform us?
Subpoint 1	We have access to God's literal words. *16 All Scripture is breathed out by God . .*

Explanation

The Bible uses phrases and words that are not natural to us. The original audience would understand them, but they seem a little funky now. I said to my wife, "I'm breathing out the grocery list." She might call a doctor. Context clues would suggest that by "breathing out," I meant to tell her the grocery list, aloud. In part of the verse, Paul is saying that all Scripture (the sixty-six books of the Bible) are the very words spoken out by God. "Breathed out" means expulsion of air by the lungs. This is God's spoken Word! (Hold up the Bible) This right here is God's actual Words! The Holy Spirit spoke out the words to the authors who wrote it down!

If this is true, it changes everything. And let me stop and say, IT IS TRUE! Since that is reality, it comes with certain implications. First, we can read the actual words of the Creator of the universe. If the president wrote you a letter, you would read it, no matter who you voted for. Well, you have the words of God right here. And since it is His words, it carries authority. We do not read God's Word to ignore it, that would be foolishness! Especially because it reveals the salvation of God.

Illustration

My first few years in college were rough. I would rather go out with friends than go to school. This mentality led to five colleges in two years with a lot of school debt. One school where I got academically relieved of my duties was Arizona State University. If you know ASU, you know that it is virtually impossible to get academically kicked out of the school. That first semester, I learned that I could do the nearly impossible. I didn't buy books, and I barely went to classes. At the end of the semester, my GPA was less than 1. Then I got a letter from the registrar signed by the dean saying something to this effect: "College might not be for you. Don't come back." That might not be a direct quote, but it was something similar. I couldn't ignore this note and just start going back to school. Why? Because the dean and the registrar had the authority to remove me from ASU. There were words that carried weight. What they said was implemented. I read it with finality.

We can easily understand the authority of a school official, but why are we so flippant about the Word of God? We read it like a hobby. We write notes and commitments we never intend to follow through on. We live as if these words do not have authority, yet they are the ultimate authority.

Application

You have the voice of God written down on pages. Are you using it? If you fail to plan, you plan to fail. So, make a plan to read daily. Set a time and place and get the discipline to follow through. I promise you will not be the same if you do. We can easily understand the authority of a school official, but why are we so flippant about the Word of God? We read it like a hobby. We write notes and commitments we never intend to follow through on. We live as if these words do not have authority, yet they are the ultimate authority.

Subpoint 2	God's Word guides us to be different. *and profitable for teaching, for reproof, for correction, and for training in righteousness...*

Explanation

God does not waste His words. Every word in the Bible has power and meaning. It is there intentionally. Paul calls it "profitable." It is not a waste. Some of you had a lemonade stand growing up. Your parents paid twenty dollars to get you the supplies. Helped you set up. And you made a whole five dollars in return. That is not profitable. That is a waste. (Yes, I know the experience might be worth it, stick with me.) The Bible is not a waste.

So, if the Bible is not a waste, what is it good for? Well Paul starts by saying it is good for teaching. This is good doctrine. Bad doctrine and false teaching were a major issue in the church. Almost every New Testament book speaks to false teaching. It was an issue then, and it is an issue now. Look at the Prosperity Gospel preached by many modern teachers. A Gospel that says if you give money to the church or a person, God will bless you with health, wealth, and prosperity. In reality, it is sending people to Hell by the thousands. The Bible does not stop at teaching, it reproofs us. Reproofing is the exposing of error. Telling us when we are wrong. We all love that, right? Well, we should start loving it. Proverbs 12:1 states: "Whoever loves discipline loves knowledge, but he who hates reproof is stupid." That's pretty clear. But what do you do when you're told you're wrong? You change! The Bible is good for correction. Experiencing reproof without correction is a waste of time. That means we have to want to change. Lastly, the Bible is good for training in righteousness. This is the process of sanctification. This is the goal of the Christian. To want to be more like Christ. The Bible trains us to be more like Christ.

The truth is the Bible does not leave anyone the same. Hebrews 4:12 says, *"For the word of God is living and active, sharper than any two-edged sword, piercing to the division of soul and of spirit, of joints and of marrow, and discerning the thoughts and intentions of the heart."* God's Word guides us to be different. But we have to want to be different.

Illustration

For ninety-five percent of my life, I've had no desire to go to the gym. I like my life as it is. Why do I want to be sore and hurt? My wife seems to like how I look. Then my late thirties hit. I was struggling with what seemed like the easiest physical tasks. I knew that I had to make a change or else I would stay the same and hurt more. So, I started making a plan.

The Stuff at the End

Application

We need a plan! Now, what should you do while reading? Well, I forget things easily and often. The only way I remember is to write down the stuff I need to remember. So, let's do that. Create a journal this week with what you've learned and your next action steps. Use 2 Timothy 3:16,17 as your guide. Ask yourself three questions every day: What is God teaching me? Where is God reproofing me? How do I correct the reproof? As we obey His Word, we start living as God intended us.

Subpoint 3	God's Word leads us to live as God intended. *17 that the man of God may be complete, equipped for every good work.*

Explanation

It would be all about us if we read verse 16 without 17. The Christian walk is not all about us. It is about God's impact on the world and how He uses us to make that impact. It's our living how God intended us to live from the start before we screwed it up with sin. Our sin (the sin from Adam and Eve) broke the world. It brought death, physical and spiritual, to the world. We are not righteous, and we are not complete. But the Bible leads us to righteousness through the salvation of Jesus Christ. He makes us complete. The Bible reveals salvation! The Bible leads us to salvation!

This is the redemptive single story of Scripture. God creates the world perfect. Adam and Eve sin and bring death and brokenness. We inherit that sin, and we continue to perpetuate that brokenness through our sin. This sin causes us to be spiritually dead. It is the punishment for sin. But God sends His son as a baby, born to a virgin. The son, Jesus, lives a perfect life, but is sent to a sinner's cross to die. His death was not unplanned. Instead, His death was the plan all along. He died to take our punishment for our sins. Then, He defeated sin in the resurrection. And after spending time with His followers, He ascended to Heaven, promising to come back. The Bible tells us the truth, spoken to us by God Himself. If you are not a follower of Jesus, today is the day. Romans 10:9,10 says, "Because, if you confess with your mouth that Jesus is Lord and believe in your heart that God raised him from the dead, you will be saved. For with the heart, one believes and is justified, and with the mouth, one confesses and is saved." In a second, I will give you the opportunity to call out to Jesus for salvation; don't waste this time.

When we are saved, we are complete. That completion is shown through our good works. The Bible equips us for those good works. It is our instruction manual on how to serve the world. This is how we live as God intended. We help heal the brokenness of the world. We live on a mission to bring the Gospel to the world!

Illustration

My desire to change and hit the gym was strong, but there was a problem: I didn't know how to do anything. I didn't know how to bench-press or squat, and I didn't know where to start. I could barely run. So, I found people in the church to teach me. I went with them to the gym and learned what each lift was and how to do it properly. We encouraged each other by text, and I learned from them.

Church, I don't expect you to naturally know how to bring the Gospel to the world or act like a follower of Jesus. Instead, we are trained by His Word. We can't do it alone!

Application

The Bible is the beautiful story of God redeeming His people. So, are you one of His people? Are you saved? Are you a follower of Jesus? If the answer is no, today is the day. At the end of the sermon, you will have an opportunity to respond to the call of Jesus.

If you are a follower, if someone looked at your life, would they know? Do you look more like the world or like Jesus? If I asked your five closest friends what was most important in your life, what would they say? How we live and what we do shows the world that we follow Jesus. If our lives are saturated with the Word of God, we will be serving others. We are doing the good works that we are equipped to do. That means our primary responsibility will be sharing the Gospel with a broken world.

Next Steps

1. Daily, thank God for giving us His Word.
2. Create a daily reading and journaling plan.
3. If you don't know Jesus, today is the day.

Outro

When I go visit my hometown, I often drive by that building. The new owners repaired and left that old sign. I often think about what that old building would look like now if it had not been transformed. See, buildings do not lie stagnant. They are either in a constant state of rebuilding or in decay. The elements of the world do not allow stagnation. And that is true for our own life. You may think that you can maintain yourselves in the same state, but you can't. You are either in a state of decay or transforming to be like Christ. While this transformation is being executed by the Holy Spirit, His primary means of that transformation is the Bible. That means you are either reading, studying, and applying Scripture or watching your spiritual walk erode. Don't waste this time. If you are not a follower of Jesus, repent and believe. Allow God to transform you into a new creation. Allow God to further your transformation through His Word. If you are a follower of Jesus, live in His Word and see the fruit that God produces through our transformation.

Prayer	• For people to follow Jesus • For us to submit to God's Word.

APPENDIX I

Standing on the Shoulders of Giants

To get the most out of this book, you need to know the places and people that influenced me. I am an amalgamation of all the people whom God has placed in my life. God has been kind to include these people and influences. Some of these I have never met but only read their work. Others have walked me through some of the toughest times in my life. If you see a book, read it. Find a sermon of one of these people and watch it.

1. **Aaron Norwood:** My friend and pastor who walked me through the first ten years of ministry. He taught me to love the Bible and preach only from it. He taught me that pastoring is much more than preaching.

2. **Brian Bowman**, Pastor at Valley Life Church, Phoenix, Arizona: Brian is one of my closest friends. He gave me the original version of the "Answer the Questions"

section of this book. I have since modified it, but his influence is still there.

3. **Dr. Nathan Millican**, Pastor at Graceland Church, Indiana: Nate is a dear friend. He has also allowed me to try all of these methods and training out on his campus pastors. That takes a lot of trust.

4. **Dr. Adam Bailey**, Pastor at Christ Church, [CITY?], Arizona: I was a part of Vintage Mission, a great network of churches around the world that Adam leads. He is a dedicated expositor of the text. Many of my ideas on preaching started through his training.

5. **Kirk Van Maanan**, Pastor at Christ Church and Director of Vintage Mission: I am proud to say Kirk is a friend of mine, although it is often one-sided. Kirk spent way too much time reviewing my sermons and writing me feedback. But it was that time and effort that allowed me to get better. He took a dull butter knife and turned it into the slightly sharper butter knife you see today.

6. **Simeon Trust Workshop**, simeontrust.org.

7. **Duvall and Hays,** Authors of *Grasping God's Word*: Read it. Learn a proper hermeneutic. The book changed my life and ministry.

There are many more people who have influenced me, but these are the ones who also influenced this book. Go see for yourselves.

APPENDIX II

Pray Psalm 119

Psalm 119

1 Blessed are those whose way is blameless,
who walk in the law of the LORD!
2 Blessed are those who keep his testimonies,
who seek him with their whole heart,

9 How can a young man keep his way pure?
By guarding it according to your word.

11 I have stored up your word in my heart,
that I might not sin against you.

20 My soul is consumed with longing.
for your rules at all times.

Simple Sermons

24 Your testimonies are my delight;
they are my counselors.

34 Give me understanding, that I may keep your law
and observe it with my whole heart.
35 Lead me in the path of your commandments,
for I delight in it.

41 Let your steadfast love come to me, O LORD,
your salvation according to your promise;
42 then shall I have an answer for him who taunts me,
for I trust in your word.

57 The LORD is my portion;
I promise to keep your words.

81 My soul longs for your salvation;
I hope in your word.

89 Forever, O LORD, your word
is firmly fixed in the heavens.

97 Oh how I love your law!
It is my meditation all the day.

114 You are my hiding place and my shield;
I hope in your word.

Pray Psalm 119

123 My eyes long for your salvation
and for the fulfillment of your righteous promise.

146 I call to you; save me,
that I may observe your testimonies.

175 Let my soul live and praise you,
and let your rules help me.
176 I have gone astray like a lost sheep; seek your servant,
for I do not forget your commandments.

Liturgy as Meditation

Daily Morning Prayer

Let the words of my mouth and the meditation of my heart be always acceptable in your sight, O Lord, my rock and my redeemer.

Psalm 19:14

Confession of Sin

Let us humbly confess our sins to Almighty God.

Almighty and most merciful Father,
we have erred and strayed from your ways like lost sheep.
We have followed too much the devices and desires of our own hearts.
We have offended against your holy laws.
We have left undone those things which we ought to have done,
and we have done those things which we ought not to have done;
and apart from your grace, there is no health in us.
O Lord, have mercy upon us.
Spare all those who confess their faults.

Restore all those who are penitent, according to your promises declared to all people in Christ Jesus our Lord.
And grant, O most merciful Father, for his sake, that we may now live a godly, righteous, and sober life, to the glory of your holy Name. Amen.
Grant to your faithful people, merciful Lord, pardon and peace; that we may be cleansed from all our sins and serve you with a quiet mind; through Jesus Christ our Lord. Amen.

Text for the Sermon

2 Timothy 3:16, 17

> **16** *All Scripture is breathed out by God and profitable for teaching, for reproof, for correction, and for training in righteousness,* **17** *that the man of God may be complete, equipped for every good work.*

The Apostles' Creed

I believe in God, the Father almighty,
creator of heaven and earth.
I believe in Jesus Christ, his only Son, our Lord.
He was conceived by the Holy Spirit
and born of the Virgin Mary.
He suffered under Pontius Pilate,
was crucified, died, and was buried.
He descended to the dead.
On the third day he rose again.
He ascended into heaven,
and is seated at the right hand of the Father.
He will come again to judge the living and the dead.
I believe in the Holy Spirit,
the holy catholic Church,
the communion of saints,
the forgiveness of sins,
the resurrection of the body,
and the life everlasting. Amen.

Preaching Preparation Document

Series:
Text:
Sermon Date:

1. What's the Big Idea?
2. Tweet the point: (180 characters or less)
   This is the one that most people struggle with. The idea is that we can succinctly state the sermon in a way that catches the listener.
3. What do you want them to know?
4. What do you want them to feel?
5. What do you want them to do?
6. What is the context?
7. What would people lose if this text weren't there?
8. How does this connect to the Gospel?
9. Big Idea Question we are answering:
10. What are the subpoints?

Bible Verses	
Verse Diagram	
Exegetical Outline	
Big Idea	
Points	
Applicational Outline	
Big Idea	
Points	
Resources	
Exegetical	
Lexicon	
Devotional	

Sermon Outline Document

Series:	
Text:	
Sermon Date:	
Big Idea:	
Intro	
Reading	
The case for the Big Idea	
Question for the Big Idea	
Subpoint 1	
Explanation	
Illustration	
Application	
Subpoint 2	
Explanation	
Illustration	
Application	
Subpoint 3	
Explanation	
Illustration	
Application	
Next Steps	
Outro	
Prayer	

www.ingramcontent.com/pod-product-compliance
Lightning Source LLC
Chambersburg PA
CBHW070149100426
42743CB00013B/2862